## About the Author

The author has spent nearly forty-two years in mental hospitals, although he maintains that he is perfectly sane and always has been. In the first book of his adult life, *My Journey Back – Part One*, he chronicles his fight with, and eventual victory over the Devil himself. He gives this as a reason for his belief that his life is indeed that of the coming Lord God. He feels that his late mother, Mrs Dorothy Ayres, took advantage of his youth and inexperience to steal his throne in the spirit world, which he is now fighting to take back. He believes that his time in mental hospitals has been spent as a political prisoner of his late mother with the collusion of the psychiatric profession under the pretext of 'mental illness', which is their way of conspiring to hide the truth. The truth is stranger than fiction, but is revealed in this author's books.

# My Journey Back – Part Two

## The Arrival of God's Kingdom

**Robert Brooks Strong**

# My Journey Back – Part Two

## The Arrival of God's Kingdom

Olympia Publishers
*London*

**www.olympiapublishers.com**
OLYMPIA PAPERBACK EDITION

A CIP catalogue record for this title is
available from the British Library.

ISBN: 978-1-78830-059-9

The names of many of the people and places in this book have
been changed to protect their identity.

First Published in 2019

Olympia Publishers
60 Cannon Street
London
EC4N 6NP

Printed in Great Britain

## Acknowledgments

I wish to acknowledge that the fact that actress, Lucy Lawless, has done nothing to imply my thoughts of her. Lucy Lawless is a person for whom one can have only the highest regard.

# Chapter 1
## The Quest for Justice

**Monday 23<sup>rd</sup> May 2016.** Welcome to *My Journey Back —
Part Two*. From now on I am chronicling events as they
transpire and my knowledge of things worth knowing as the
realisations occur to me. I am doing this in the form of a diary
but I do not think I will be making an entry every day – just
when I have something worth writing about.

I am still a patient in a psychiatric hospital but even my
fellow patients are speculating on where I go from here.
Yesterday an old friend suggested I try to get a place in a
hospital in Wales, which would be a green and pleasant place
for me to see out my days. When I mentioned this at the
communal meal we have on this ward on Sundays, someone
else suggested I try for a discharge and buy myself a house in
one of the Welsh valleys. Property is cheap in the old mining
districts where the miners have vacated their houses and
moved away because of the demise of the coal industry in this
country.

I have enough money saved up for a three-bedroom semi,
which will need some renovation. I have a meeting next month
called a 'CPA' meeting, at which most of the people who
affect my life have their say, then invite me to have my say. I
am going to suggest to these people that if I get a discharge, I
will be able to look after myself in my own house. I will have
a couple of bedrooms spare, so I can have the company of a
couple of fee-paying guests, which will give me a retirement
income.

Those who have read *My Journey Back – Part One*, will know that I am waiting for the actress, Lucy Lawless, to take an interest in me and write back to me, which she has never done. I have been waiting for her since 1999 when I first wrote to her. I have dug my heels in over Lucy being my choice of partner, although my mother wants me to go with a girl named Rebecca. It is a long time since my mother was able to tell me what to do, especially in something as important as my choice of wife.

**Wednesday 25th May 2016**. My twelve complimentary copies of *My Journey There* arrived on the ward on Monday and this has caused quite a stir. I am keeping one for myself and giving a copy to my nearest relatives and a few to staff here at the hospital. That is my plan but I will have to get permission from the multi-disciplinary team meeting today to do what I want to do. That is the way of most things here, we have to go through the MDT to get permission to breathe.

I have been told that both my responsible clinician and my social worker are absent today, so the MDT has been postponed for a week. I asked my ward manager for a decision on who I can give copies of my book to and she told me that they are holding a meeting early next week to discuss my book, including the decision on who I can give copies to.

My primary nurse is also absent today. She is a very nice lady but still a lot younger than me so when I explain myself, she doesn't understand and assumes I am mentally ill. Like a lot of people round here, they are in for a shock when they discover who I really am. The psychiatric system is very reluctant to let go of someone they find interesting. All I want from them is to come off medication, because I have no sex life at all whilst I am on the drug. It also contributes to the pains I feel in my hips and legs. As I have said before, those who force people to take antipsychotic drugs against that person's will, shall be coming back as rats in their next life.

Not many of the psychiatrists who do this to people have ever taken the 'medication' themselves, so they have no idea of what they are doing to people. What they are really doing is bullying people into taking the politically correct attitude, and trying to frighten people who have the guts to speak their mind.

**Friday 27th May 2016.** I suffer greatly from pain in my hips and my legs. It is worst at night and first thing in the morning. I think it is a combination of osteoarthritis and sciatica. I have already asked my primary nurse to mention this at the next MDT meeting. Three years ago (2013) I had a bad spell of sciatica and the only thing that helped me was acupuncture. I am going to contact the lady again for some more acupuncture sessions, assuming I am allowed to.

I usually go to bed between 7 pm and 8 pm and I am usually asleep by 8 pm. I usually wake up in the small hours of the morning and wait until at least 3 am before getting up. Life is a strange business when your soulmate lives on the other side of the world! It is just as well I am retired and I can choose my sleeping habits to please myself. I usually have a nap in the afternoon as well. I normally sleep on top of the bed but the nights have been so cold lately that I have to get under the duvet to get some relief from the cold. The maintenance people have put the night time central heating back on, which is a relief. They had turned it off on the assumption that summer had arrived. They really should know the English summer better!

Over the last few weeks, I have been attending a hospital for problems to do with my waterworks. I had to spend eight days as an inpatient when I got an infection that needed an antibiotic drip 24/7. I was linked up to the antibiotics as well as some saline solution which was input into my urinary works. I had a three-way catheter on my penis for most of the eight days and now I have been out of hospital for a month or so, I can't urinate normally at all! I have to use a catheter to empty my bladder, which I do three or four times a day. I'm due for an operation on my bladder in August, so I'm hoping that will solve the problem for good. It stems from the fact that

I have an unusually large bladder and the doctors say that after the operation it will be reduced to normal size, and hopefully normal function.

I am a singer/songwriter/guitarist and I've got two concerts coming up early next month, so I really must get round to rehearsing my numbers. When I do these gigs, I usually alternate between one of my own songs and a song which is a cover version of a song by a more celebrated artiste. I have a full repertoire of over a hundred songs in my head, thirty-nine of which are my own compositions, but a one-hour gig only gives time for about seventeen songs, so I have divided my repertoire into four sets of twenty or so songs each, and I do one set per concert. I usually do the same set at the nursing home as I do at a close date to my concert here at Alcatraz Island. Both venues ask for me monthly, so I rehearse the same set for each venue on the month, and the next set on the next month etcetera.

So what with my autobiography, my concerts and this diary, I lead quite a full life. I have a few unfulfilled wishes, one of which is full access to the internet. If I had that, I could upload my songs onto websites such as Amazon and Apple i-tunes and make my songs available to the record buying public. I'm sure some of my thirty-nine songs would be hits.

My main unfulfilled wish is to get Lucy Lawless to enter a relationship with me, even if it's only as pen pals.

**Tuesday 31st May 2016**. I have sent out two copies of *My Journey There;* one to my son, Christopher and one to Lucy Lawless. Those two were important to me but I am waiting until I get permission from the MDT, tomorrow, before sending out the remaining copies. I have written to the lady in the Marketing and Promotion department at Olympia Publishers, asking who is going to stock copies of my book. I have been told that people interested can buy it from Amazon but I am still waiting for news about other bookshops.

Earlier this month I hired a recording studio for a morning and recorded some songs of my own composition. It is over two weeks now since I had my recording session at ORIOL'S and I still haven't received my disks. I think I shall have to write to Adam to chastise him. I recorded an album of twenty of my songs and a disk with three songs on it, these being the songs I have written since my recording sessions at Broadmoor, when I recorded thirty-six of my songs. I now have three disks with my total of thirty-nine songs on them. I wish I could start selling them.

**Thursday 2<sup>nd</sup> June 2016**. I heard on the telly yesterday that one of the symptoms of Motor Neurone Disease is slurred speech. My speech has been slurred for some time now, even when I was on a drug called Paliperidone. I am now on a drug called Aripiprazole which makes it worse. I put it down to the drug having a similar effect to alcohol, but now I am not so sure. I am thinking that it may be that I have been given Motor Neurone Disease from the neuroleptic drugs that I have been forced to take and still am. I hope to see my primary nurse about this today.

I always thought that if I was successful in my fight for justice, I would have a role to play as public hero, which is how I see myself. I don't want to hide behind a veil of anonymity like my parents before me and various other people before them. In ages to come, I want people to use the phrase 'When God walked the Earth''. In the future, members of the psychiatric profession won't be just tolerated as figures of ridicule, like they are today, but they will be passionately hated as the people who hated the Lord.

**Friday 3<sup>rd</sup> June 2016**. I am due to attend a meeting of the Patient's Council this afternoon. I am the secretary so I must be there. They would be lost without me. I will be scribbling down the minutes of the meeting as they occur, then tomorrow I shall type them up nicely and arrange for them to be circulated to all who attended the meeting, plus the hospital directors.

When I was considering whether or not my late mother forfeit her humanity, I took into account the notion that you reap what you sow, and there is nothing worse I can think of for myself than to lose my humanity. This has meant sharing power to a large extent with my mother. Those who regard compassion as a weakness will not follow me, but those who know it is a strength will follow me to the ends of the Earth for eternity. I am still human though and it is human nature to want to be the one who gives the orders rather than the one who carries them out. Consequently, I have decided in my mind upon a compromise, and one I am entering here in writing for all to read. If I get justice for myself by the end of this year, then my mother's position in the firmament will be permanent. But if January 1st 2017 dawns and justice still looks no nearer, then I will not rest until I have brought my mother's soul back in the body of a goose.

I repeat, by 'justice' I want four things: -

1. FREEDOM
2. APOLOGY
3. EXONERATION
4. COMPENSATION

My mother is the one who is on trial now. Either I get justice or she loses her humanity. Either way she has got until the end of this calendar year to prove to me that she really does care.

I am going to close this chapter here. It leaves a lot of balls in the air, both those of my mother and those of my sweetheart, Lucy. Also my custodians. I have a case review this month, here they call these reviews 'CPA' meetings. It suits me to spend some more time in here at the moment. This place is like a fortress and offers me protection from the paparazzi. I just wish they would take me off the accursed medication. There is no need to take the cover so realistically.

# Chapter 2
## Royalties on Books

**Sunday 5th June 2016.** I have stopped trying to solve the riddle of Lucy's behaviour. It seems that whatever solution I come up with, something else turns out to be even more likely. It must be Lucy's mind at work, thwarting my efforts to get to know her. I had a similar sort of experience years ago when I realised that it was the fact of my wanting something that stopped me from getting it. It turned out to be my mother's influence at work having a game with me and the whole of society in Britain was in on the joke.

I've decided to follow my own instincts. Forty years ago, I used to tell my sons that if they wanted to interest a girl in them, then to follow the example of the birds. A bird will build a nest first and then reveal his plumage. The female bird will then choose her mate from the best nests on offer, as well as the most attractive plumage. I had my own house at the time and I had trouble keeping the girls away. To relate this to my present situation, I have heard that one can buy a three-bedroom semi-detached house in the Welsh Valleys for about £20,000. It will need another £15,000 spending on it to get it shipshape but I can manage that.

The old mining villages in the Welsh valleys are now deserted as the coal mines have all been closed and the miners have had to move to the cities, leaving their houses abandoned. The houses are now going so cheaply because there is no employment in these districts. This to me is a golden opportunity to buy houses, do them up and then sell or let them to retired people who are not looking for employment. The mining villages could come back to life as retirement villages and there is scope here to build golf courses and other activities to interest retired folk. The natural beauty of the Welsh countryside is an added bonus to anyone who wants to live in the Welsh valleys.

I shall put these ideas to the CPA meeting which takes place later this month and hope that wheels can be put in motion to give me a discharge so that I may put my ideas into practice.

**Monday 6<sup>th</sup> June 2016.** I get a lot of hints that 'the code' is responsible for Lucy's behaviour but I haven't got the time or the inclination to fathom out what is meant by 'the code'. In any event, I am fed up with playing guessing games. I've had a belly full of them over the past few years and I'm just not interested anymore. I've made my play for Lucy and by now she should know whether or not she wants me. If she does, then it's up to her to let me know and play it straight with me. If she doesn't do that then I shall have to assume there is nothing I can do to interest her and make other plans for myself.

In any event, although I am now seventy-two years of age, I sill intend to buy a house in the Welsh valleys and do it up myself. I'm sure there will be plenty of females who will like what I will then have to offer. I'm following my own advice about the birds and the bees and I would like a nest in place to offer, as a gambit in the mating game.

I did manage an orgasm recently, just when I thought I was saying 'goodbye' to sexual activity. There are still plenty of women who want to dance with me, and there is plenty of life in this old dog yet. I am still very attractive for a man of my age, and I intend to play that to the full.

**Thursday 9<sup>th</sup> June 2016.** On Tuesday I put on a concert at The old folks Nursing Home and did quite a bit of shopping as well, both before and after the concert. As a result of Monday's entry, I feel Lucy's love very strongly. I feel that Lucy and I are closer together than other people who know each other socially but lack a spiritual bond. I feel happy knowing that Lucy and I are part of each other.

I get the impression that many people still want me to crack the code that restricts Lucy. Wherever I go I get signs that it will be worth my while to crack this code. I bought a frozen meal for one on Tuesday and when I read the instructions for cooking it, it transpired that I have to have some involvement with 'the code'. I haven't cooked it yet, nor fully read the information about their code, as Peter, the painter, came along and asked me to leave the kitchen as he was about to recommence painting it. He'll finish it before tonight so I'll have another look at the 'Bisto' frozen meal code! I feel confident that I can crack this code and win Lucy.

We who live on The Rehab Ward, Alcatraz Island, enjoy the privilege of being able to cook for ourselves but we can't do it today because of the fact that Peter is painting the kitchen. We have to eat in the communal dining hall today, and get our food from the main kitchens. I don't mind as the food there isn't too bad usually, and I'll save a few bob on the cost of a meal.

I got some papers in the post on Tuesday telling me that if I complete their form and hand it in by 30th June then I'll be eligible for my share of royalties on public library books borrowed from libraries. It certainly seems that Olympia are not pulling any punches when it comes to marketing my book, *My Journey There*. It is in their interest for as many people to buy it as they can get to do so. This means I am rubbing my hands with glee. I have got to reach £2,500 in royalties before I break even. I get the feeling that it is going to make me a lot of money. This will enable me to create a beautiful nest for my mate, Lucy.

My primary nurse here is called Daisy and she is on leave, so this afternoon I am seeing a nurse called Freida, to get some help with the paperwork involved in completing this form. It is not straightforward. It may involve a letter from Dr Marionette Madre to establish my identity. I have only got until 30th June so I can't hang about. The pace of life here in

Hampshire is much slower than London and I am still used to getting things done pronto, because time is money.

I made an important realisation today. If I am wondering what to do with someone who has both points for them and points against them, then the best road I can take is to set them a test. I reached this realisation by extrapolating to the general from the specific. I have been wondering what to do with my late mother. I have set her a trial, to prove if she really does love me or not. I know she hates the idea of forfeiting her human identity, so the trial will have both a stick and a carrot.

She still has enormous indirect influence on current affairs in Great Britain. I want her to use that influence to get me the four things I want by way of justice from British society. I have given her a timeline for this, and that is by the end of this calendar year. If the 1st January 2017 dawns and I am no nearer getting justice, then I will turn my late mother's soul into a goose egg and she will hatch out as a gosling. If, on the other hand, I have achieved the four things I want by way of justice, then her position in the hierarchy of souls of the human race will be assured. What happens now is up to her.

**Friday 10th June 2016.** Young Freida helped me with the public library application for royalties form. It only remains now for my charge nurse to sign, saying she has known me for two years. My charge nurse is a woman called Portia. She is an incredibly forceful woman. Some may say a 'battle-axe'. I don't like the attitude she often takes with me, but at other times she is as nice as can be. I guess she has problems of her own.

My primary nurse, Daisy, has a way with Portia and she is also very good with me. She pretends to understand the things I tell her, draws her own conclusions (namely that I am mentally ill), then reports her findings to Marionette Madre. I have a case conference on Wednesday of next week. Here they call it a 'Care Plan Approach' meeting (CPA). I hope to persuade them that it is time now for some kind of discharge for me. I shall explain to them the details of housing in the

Welsh valleys and hope they see my plan as realistic. No one thought I could get my autobiography published until I succeeded in doing so. I believe I mentioned in one of my earlier writings, that greatness lies in doing things that most people think no one has the balls to do. Greatness is often mistaken for madness, especially within a man's own lifetime. Paul Simon wrote a song called *The sound of Silence*. I am the man who dared disturb the sound of silence. I did so forty years ago when I killed Iris.

I've just returned to the ward from the dining hall. Today, being Friday, we had fish and chips. It wasn't too bad but you can hardly ever get a nice piece of cod these days. I spoke to Portia about her signature on the document that Freida helped me with yesterday and Portia told me that she is leaving it for Daisy to sign. Daisy isn't due back at work until Tuesday of next week! Part of Portia's problem seems to me that she cannot read English very well. She declined the opportunity to read my manuscript or the finished book of *My Journey There*.

I don't know where Portia comes from. One of the patients told me that he thinks she is Egyptian. I was offered another chance to criticise the book today but I am content that Olympia are working hard in the sales and promotion department. What lines their pockets, lines mine so I'm glad I've got them on my side. My job is done as far as *My Journey There* is concerned; I wrote the book; I did all the proofreading; I worked with their illustrator to produce a brilliant front cover. Now all I have to do is sit back and watch the money roll in. When it gets to £2,500 I shall break even and after that it will be all profit, except for the huge cost of time and stationery. It has been one hell of an adventure for myself and also the publishers. The publishers must have costed their efforts, so now they too will be keeping a weather eye open on sales.

I am waiting until I have a few thousand quid more than I possess at the moment before I engage a solicitor to launch my claim for justice in the courts. I am doing it this way because I can't afford to pay legal fees and buy a house out of my one pot of money. I've got just over £35,000 to my name but I'll need a lot more to cover legal fees. In the meantime, though, I'm keeping a lookout for a firm of solicitors who can represent me well in my fight for justice. I'm hoping that the sales of *My Journey There* will create a mood of public sympathy for myself and my cause which will help me get the four things I want from society.

Namely:   1.   FREEDOM.   2.   APOLOGY.   3. EXONERATION. 4. COMPENSATION. I intent to live the rest of my life as a public hero, which is what I deserve for overcoming the Devil himself and freeing mankind from Him forever!

I'm sure that if I am well off financially it will help me attract Lucy into my life.

**Sunday 12th June 2016**. I put on a concert in The Sunlight Room yesterday. I had an audience of seven patients and two staff and I performed set three of my repertoire, plus I handled a couple of requests; one for a Bob Dylan number and one for a Paul Simon song. The afternoon was very successful. They clapped at the end of each song and I also got a round of applause at the end of the show. The show only lasted an hour, from 3 pm to 4 pm but that is long enough for a solo artiste to perform.

I'm still waiting for Adam of ORIOL'S to deliver my disks. It was 20th May that I recorded them. I paid him £75 for the use of his facilities for a morning. He should have ten disks for me and he promised Brenda McQueen (my occupational therapist) that he would deliver them here on Fridy 10th June, but he was not as good as his word.

I think I'll practise my electric guitar this afternoon. I'm learning a new piece called *Nashville Boogie*. This will also give me the opportunity to try out my new music stand. I have really progressed as a musician in the last couple of years, thanks to my music tutor who is both a good musician and a good teacher.

We will be having a take-away meal this evening, which I am looking forward to and James O'Toole is the name of the guy who takes the orders and organises everything. I've got to wait an hour before James surfaces and takes the orders. That will be 11 am after which I will have a light lunch to keep me going until the take-away this evening.

**Tuesday 14<sup>th</sup> June 2016.** I'm a bit upset because Daisy isn't back from her leave yet and I need her signature on the application form for royalties on books borrowed from public libraries. The form must be handed in by the end of this month, otherwise I shall have to wait another year, so I hope Daisy gets back to work soon. Portia doesn't want to know about it and is leaving it to Daisy. She won't even tell me when Daisy will be back at work, which she should know as the clinical team leader.

I am going to close this chapter here because I have had a realisation that I wish to start a new chapter with.

# Chapter 3
# Mountains

**Tuesday 14<sup>th</sup> June 2016**. I think Lucy has received her copy of *My Journey There*. It occurred to me today that both Lucy and I have been given mountains to climb in order to get to each other. Lucy has this horrible code to break the spell of, whilst I have to extricate myself from neuroleptic drugs and detention at the hands of the psychiatric profession.

There was a man in America who wrote a song called *This Time you gave me a Mountain*. I guess the present situation is his revenge and that of many like-minded people. My thoughts are, 'Just watch our smoke, folk and we'll show you how a real man and a real woman do it!'

Lucy and I are one being, we have a spiritual bond of love and understanding far stronger than most married couples, even though we have never met in person.

I had an offer from Olympia Publishers today, to publish *My Journey Back*. What they failed to realise was that I am only offering part one for publication at this time, I am still writing part two. I must now write to them again and point this out.

**Wednesday 15<sup>th</sup> June 2016**. It is 2.56 in the morning and it is very cold, too cold to sleep, so I have already washed and dressed myself and got ready for the day. I will be going to the kitchen to make my first cup of coffee of the day in one hour's time but for now I have some things to write about.

It is my CPA meeting this afternoon, so I hope to sow the seeds of thinking about my discharge in their minds. I had hoped to discuss the future with Lucy and make plans for where we want to live and what we want to do with the rest of our lives together. I am going to inform the meeting of my plans to buy a house in one of the Welsh valleys that used to be the house of a coal miner, but the miners have all abandoned their houses and moved to the cities now that coal mining is an obsolete profession, just as my skills in data processing are now also obsolete. It is a fast-changing world.

However, I have enough money to buy a house in one of the Welsh valleys and renovate it. I have been reliably informed that one can buy a three-bedroom semi for £20,000 and renovate it for a further £15,000. I have enough money to do this and I have also got money to come from my writing and my music. My future looks bright and I am sure it will attract Lucy, once the code is broken and we have got together.

**Thursday 16th June 2016**. The CPA meeting went very well yesterday. Dr Marionette Madre made some very encouraging remarks concerning giving me a drug-free trial period. I pray that this will happen. The Paliperidone has now almost completely worked its way out of my system and I am feeling better for this. I am still on the tablets of Aripiprazole but they aren't as bad as the injections. My buttocks and arms are still getting over all the years of injections.

I think I have both arthritis and sciatica in my hips. They hurt like hell, and so do my legs. I have booked another appointment with the acupuncturist, and I will be visiting her in two weeks' time for an acupuncture session. I know from experience that the first two sessions of a course of acupuncture make the pain worse, but after that it gets better quickly. Western medicine has nothing to offer for sciatica.

**Saturday 18th June 2016**. My primary nurse, Daisy, returned from holiday yesterday and I gave her some work to do on my behalf. I want that young woman to understand me. She has already accepted that I am the King. She said so in no uncertain terms when she took me to hospital in Brixton a couple of months ago. She persuaded me to sit in the largest chair in the waiting room and when I said that it needed a very large man to occupy that chair, she said, "You're the King, Bob." A little recognition goes a long way.

On Thursday, one of my fellow patients, called James Taylor, and I went to a place in Wolverhampton to buy ourselves a new chair each. We both chose the liner/recliner, which is very comfortable and has two electric motors! One for the footrest to rise and one for the back and seat to rise to let you get to your feet without too much trouble. I originally wanted my chair in leather but I accepted that leather would be too hot in summer and too cold in winter, so I took this advice and chose a very durable and beautiful fabric instead. It was Daisy that wanted me to have a luxurious chair as she likes to thinks of me on a throne, as do a lot of people. I do hope we can avoid a clash between my status and that of the 'royal' family because that would result in another civil war. I think it is my job to be the uncrowned king, without the status, but with most of the power and influence, whilst the monarch has all the recognition but whose role is almost completely ceremonial. When and if it comes to a fight to see who is the real boss, then that is MY job, as all my dead rivals will testify.

**Sunday 19<sup>th</sup> June 2016**. Daisy is back at work now and I have given her a few things to do which will help her to an understanding of what is really going on.

Genghis Khan had his boyhood friend killed because, as the friend himself said, "There can only be one sun in the sky." That poor man knew his fate and he knew there was nothing he could do about it.

There was a feature on the telly yesterday about the IRA and one of the bad things they did. The perpetrators of the offence were people who knew the 'code word'. So it seems to me this code that holds Lucy in its spell is nothing more than a password. I hope I discover it in time to prevent more tragedy in my life.

**Monday 20<sup>th</sup> June 2016**. I am due to go out to a Greek restaurant in Windsor. There will be two staff with me and I will be happy to buy them both a meal. When I was on the outside, forty years ago, I always used to enjoy going to Greek restaurants for a meal, especially ones with live bouzouki music.

It is now 3.45 pm and we have just returned from the Greek restaurant in Windsor. It was a smashing meal, especially for the money, but the car parking charge was exorbitant.

I had a word with Marionette Madre this morning before we left for the restaurant. Daisy had done a good job in explaining things to the doctor. She thought we should have a look on the internet to see if there is a qualified acupuncturist in Brixton or Wolverhampton. If so, then it would be a better place for me to go than Glasgow. The staff man, David, said he would look into this, so I am just waiting for him to get back to me with some details.

These trips of ours outside the hospital are called section 17 trips. I used to wonder what was the significance of the number 17. Now I know. It is the house number of the Therapeutic Clinic!

**Wednesday 22<sup>nd</sup> June 2016**. The trip to the Greek restaurant went very well. There were two staff and myself. We had a three-course meal. The food was plentiful and delicious and we thoroughly enjoyed ourselves. The bill from the restaurant came to under fifty quid, so I was well pleased. The only fly in the ointment was the charge to park the car. That cost me eight pounds for an hour and ten minutes, which I thought was extortionate.

David, the staff man, is looking up acupuncturists in Brixton and Wolverhampton and the staff have been given instructions to cancel my appointment on Thursday 30<sup>th</sup> June at the Therapeutic Clinic.

I was called to speak to the multi-disciplinary team meeting (MDT) this afternoon and Marionette was keen to offload me onto another place. She suggested a place called The Smart Clinic, near Stansted airport. It is apparently a step down to go there from Alcatraz Island. By that they apparently mean a move to even less security. I'm not sure if I would like another move but I told them I'd consider such a move and pay the place a visit. I'm keeping an open mind on the subject.

One thing I thought worth a mention concerns Motor Neurone Disease (MND). The main side effect of this disease is slurred speech. I have slurred speech, caused by the Aripiprazole, so I thought that maybe prolonged use of Aripiprazole can cause MND. I saw Dr Basil, my GP here, and she assured me that there is no way for Aripiprazole to cause MND. She seemed confident enough in her judgement so I decided to take her word for it and stop worrying about MND.

**Friday 24<sup>th</sup> June 2016**. I felt Lucy's presence as I was reading my diary this afternoon and we both were in the mood for making love, so we did it again with our minds and it was wonderful. There is no doubt in my mind that Lucy and I belong to each other – in spite of the drugs that the doctors force me to take and in spite of my jealous mother, and in spite of the code that prevents Lucy from communicating with me. This, in spite of the age difference between us, we are climbing all the mountains that the world puts in our way, knowing that what we have is worth anything and everything that the world has to offer. And that the true love we share will conquer all. We communicate in the most basic and primitive way any two souls can and nothing in the universe can stop us. We both know that it is only a question of time before we get together in the so-called 'real' world.

It is my brother, Bill's, birthday today so I sent him a card and a reminder that if he wants a complimentary copy of *My Journey There*, he has to ask me for one. That is the way my charge nurse, Portia, insists we do it. Bill is seventy-five today and going strong so I wish him all the best. I am also reserving complimentary copies for my cousin, Shaun, and my niece, Rachel. They have both been informed that they have to contact me before I can send them a copy. I wanted to give a copy of *My Journey There* to some of the staff here but Portia won't let me. She has taken the copy which I gave to David and she keeps it in her office. Then, any staff who want to read the book can borrow it from Portia.

I am considering a move to Smart House more strongly when it holds promise of getting away from Portia. There is only one of her and I would rather live in an environment without her. Maybe I will get a real adult if I have a change of hospital, although I doubt if I would get a shrink who has a beneficial attitude to neuroleptic drugs. They all believe in the drugs, like some crazy religious cult, but they don't take the damn things themselves!

**Saturday 25th June 2016**. I woke up this morning blissfully happy. What makes me happy is that I can feel Lucy's love. There is a song (I think it is by Bob Dylan) called *To Make You Feel my Love*. Adele made it popular recently. I feel as though Lucy has applied the lyrics to her feelings for me, because I can feel her love so very strongly. I didn't know it was possible for anyone to feel this good.

I'm waiting for everyone else on my scene to make their next move. There's nothing more I can do and neither Daisy nor David are in work today.

My left leg hurts like hell, especially the thigh bone and my left hip. I got the feeling that Lucy wanted to dance again today but I couldn't do it because of the pain in my leg. The problem with the leg doesn't diminish the happiness I feel, thanks to Lucy. I know I've got this feeling for ever now and that just adds to the happiness.

Who said that love was only for the young? I'll be seventy-three years young this year and I'm enjoying a love that can't be bettered. It comes from being honest with yourself, because you can't love anyone until you know yourself thoroughly. Until then you don't know what nor who is doing the loving. I think it is true that young love is blind and doomed to failure but the kids have to go through it in order to *find* themselves. Lasting love doesn't happen until you both know you've found your soulmate.

**Monday 27th June 2016.** I saw David yesterday and he told me that he had found the details of acupuncturists in Wolverhampton and Brixton and that he would be passing this information to Daisy who will then discuss it with me. I am hoping to get together with Daisy soon to discuss this.

**Tuesday 28th June 2016.** A little while ago, one of my fellow patients saw an advertisement in a newspaper for a radio-controlled talking wristwatch. He knew that would interest me, so he showed me the ad. I placed an order and the watch arrived yesterday. I am well pleased with it. The instruction leaflet is well written in largish letters for easy reading and all that you need to know is well presented. It speaks the time and, if you want it, the day and date. It cost £30 plus postage.

Daisy found an acupuncturist in Wolverhampton but she doesn't work on Tuesdays so Daisy is going to contact her again tomorrow. I was originally booked to do my week's shopping on Thursday afternoon but Daisy changed it to Wednesday morning because the date of 30th June was still too auspicious for comfort. I'll be glad when this nightmare of Lucy's entrapment is over. I am determined to free her come what may. Some things are worth dying for. Lucy's freedom is one of them as far as I am concerned. No one should threaten anyone else to the point where they are too afraid to speak or write to someone, especially a loved one.

# Chapter 4
## In the Know

**Friday 1ˢᵗ July 2016**. It is just gone two in the morning and I'm having another sleepless night. I said I would make an entry in this diary whenever I get something worth revealing. I now have such an article.

Dr Marionette Madre has told me several times that her decision to keep me on so-called 'antipsychotic' drugs was not hers alone but the decision of the whole care team. I have mentioned several times that the worst of the effects of the drugs is the suppression of the libido. I am currently on a drug call Aripiprazole. I take it in tablet form and the dosage is ten milligrams a day. It completely suppresses my sexual drive; I can't even get an erection.

One of the consequences of this is the weather in this country. Let me say why. There is no doubt that Lucy Lawless is the living embodiment of Mother Nature herself and Lucy's moods determine the weather! When she is happy, the weather is sunny and when she is sad, it is overcast with clouds which bring the rain. When I 'dance' with Lucy we get good weather and when I can't dance because of the effects of the drug we get lousy weather. This is what has been going on in Great Britain ever since Dr Madre put me on aripiprazole. We are having one of the worst summers on record.

If Dr Madre and the care team were to decide to take me off all antipsychotic drugs, then I would get my sex drive back. Lucy and I would then make love with our minds. Lucy would then be happy and the weather would consequently improve, giving us a glorious summer.

I think that one of the members of the care team is jealous of Lucy, because Lucy is my soulmate, not her. She then insists I take these horrible drugs to spite Lucy and myself. My initial reaction when I realised this was happening was to tell this person that when she dies, I will have no mercy on her soul. But I am here to judge all people and I can say to all people that the way to salvation is to confess, apologise, repent and atone for your sins. This is what I want this person to do but if she still continues with her spiteful attitude then I will probably make an example of her and subject her to my wrath.

Don't get me wrong. I am not threatening to be physically violent or break the law in any way. But there are ways by which one person can get his own back without breaking the law or being violent. My way is to expose such people to the world and to tell the world what a nasty, spiteful person they really are.

**Monday 4<sup>th</sup> July 2016.** I sent copies of the above page to my primary nurse, Daisy, and also told Dr Marionette Madre. I had a chat with Daisy about it over the weekend and Daisy asked me the name of the person in the care team whom I suspect has an ulterior motive for treating me this way. I have deliberately not mentioned her name in this narrative because it is not something that can be proven, although I am sure of it. She has got jealousy and spite written all over her face as anyone who can read people's faces will tell you.

Daisy suggested that she and Dr Madre and I have a chat about it to see what can be done. I suggested that this person and I have some sessions together as she is one of the senior psychologists in this hospital. Then I can get an idea of what to say for the best. I could then play her at her own game. Perhaps she wants a sexual relationship with me, in which case I will bury her alive so to speak. I gave Daisy her name and Daisy will report everything to Dr Marionette Madre.

Whatever the outcome of this mess, I want my sex drive back and I will reduce this person to an unrequited lover if I have to. I could and might haul her over the metaphorical coals to achieve my objective. Like I said, hold tight and observe what a real man can do.

**Tuesday 5th July 2016**. Yesterday evening, I was carrying something quite heavy up some stairs when I felt something give way at the back of my left knee. Now I find it hurts like hell when I try to bend my knee. I can just about walk, with a limp but I can't put any weight on my left leg. This problem is in addition to sciatica and osteoarthritis of the hips. I am due to see a consultant acupuncturist on Thursday afternoon so I'll be very interested to hear what he has to say.

I can still feel Lucy's love, even though I have been emasculated by the horrible drug. This proves that she loves me for myself, not just for sex, like my mother did. Which is no less than I would expect from my soulmate. She knows I still love her even though I can't do anything about it sexually at the moment. We are both doing all we can to climb the mountains that society has put in front of us.

I am now going to send a copy of this chapter of this book to Lucy Lawless, together with copies of the discs that I recorded a while ago. Lucy still hasn't heard me singing and playing my latest song, *You Tease Me*. I hope she likes it. I wrote it for her. Unfortunately, my singing voice is marred by slurred speech at the moment. It makes me sound a bit drunk, but it is just one of the nasty effects of the so-called 'antipsychotic' drugs that I am forced to take. The three songs on the smaller disk are the ones that I wrote since my recording sessions in Broadmoor, copies of which I have already sent to Lucy.

**Thursday 7th July 2016**. It is 2.43 in the morning and I am having another sleepless night. I am looking forward to the arrival of my new chair this morning. The people I am buying it from phoned to say it will be delivered this morning. The chair is called a liner/recliner and I am well pleased with it. It has two electric motors; one to raise the foot rest and one to raise the seat and back so you are lifted to the vertical when you wish to leave the chair. It is very heavy, so I have prepared a space for it in my room and vacuum cleaned my rug. I think that the delivery men will put it where I want.

31

This afternoon, I have an appointment with a consultant acupuncturist in Wolverhampton. I am sure he will agree with my diagnosis of sciatica and book me in for a course of treatment. One thing I have found with acupuncture; the pain gets worse before it gets better. It is still, however, the only known cure for sciatica. Western medicine has nothing to offer except pain-killers, which cease to work once your body gets used to them.

**Friday 8th July 2016**. Yesterday was a busy day. My chair arrived late in the morning and I was already behind schedule having been summoned to give some blood. I just had a light lunch as there wasn't time to cook and eat a meal with everything else that was going on. I didn't have time to give the chair a thorough test of all its features but I had a little go on it. I then had my Section 17 leave, which involved shopping for my week's groceries at Waitrose, then I had an appointment with the acupuncturist at 3 pm. Instead of going to Streatham for my visit to Waitrose, we went to the store in Wolverhampton which made life easier for me. Jonah, the staff man who was driving, lives in Wolverhampton so he knew the roads OK. We got everything done and arrived at the clinic with twenty minutes to spare. I was thirsty so Jonah drove me to a convenient store where I could buy a drink of fruit juice and we stepped inside the clinic at 3 pm precisely.

The acupuncturist, a chap by the name of Chris Boardman, was very competent and professional and I have great hopes that with his help I'll be sciatica free in a few weeks' time. I didn't have any of the great agony that I had in 2013 with the previous acupuncturist, but today I can feel a strong prickly sensation where Chris inserted his needles. I still walk with a limp as I can't put much weight on my left leg.

When we got back to the ward, I cooked and ate my dinner at around half past five and then I put my new chair through its paces. I am well pleased with it.

The girls and women who work in this hospital have to wear jumpers or something similar so as not to reveal any cleavage. It is assumed that a glimpse of a female breast will drive the fellas mad! My female escort yesterday afternoon was a girl named Erica. She has quite a large personal following; for example, females with her name are very popular on TV at the moment. Yesterday, Erica unbuttoned her cardigan to reveal a very nice bit of cleavage. She had just been telling me that she intends to buy herself a copy of *My Journey There*, although she hadn't heard of it until I told her about it in the car on the way to Wolverhampton. I 'danced' with Erica early this morning and thoroughly enjoyed it. I have now had two orgasms in the last week, in spite of the medication.

I felt a bit guilty dancing with Erica when Lucy is my soulmate, but a man can have a little ice cream now and again. I don't think Erica will ever be a serious rival to Lucy for my heart but I was flattered that she risked a lot to show me some cleavage.

**Saturday 9th July 2016**. I slept most of last night in my new chair! It was the comfiest sleep I've had for a long time. I have to adjust the chair to the reclining position, which also raises the footrest and Bob's your uncle! This morning I was drinking coffee while leaning back with my feet up and watching the news on telly, when the charge nurse looked in and said that I looked very posh! I've never been called that before.

I like and appreciate quality in things but not to the point of being extravagant. When people compare wristwatches and their price, mine only cost £30.00 plus postage but it keeps perfect time by radio control from the atomic clock, so I tell people that I wear a watch as a timepiece not a status symbol. That usually silences the snobs.

I'm playing in the band on Monday. The occupational therapists have organised a 'fun week' next week and on Monday afternoon we are putting on a concert. It is all good practice for me as a musician. We have a small band here. There are two of us playing rhythm guitar, one guy on keyboards, one on the tom-tom drum, a bass guitarist and a singer. The music tutor plays bass guitar and one of the occupational therapists plays keyboards, guitar and vocals. I'm now going to rehearse for Monday's concert.

**Sunday 10<sup>th</sup> July 2016**. I danced with Lucy again at 5 am this morning and our mental love making sessions just keep on getting better. I love Lucy with all my heart and mind and soul and there is nothing I wouldn't do or be for her. Whatever makes Lucy happy is what I want. I intend to lay off the ice cream in future, even though that is hard to do when so many women and girls try to impress me with their sexuality. Lucy makes me so very happy. I did not know such happiness existed before I felt Lucy's love.

The name I am going to give the person in my care team who insists I take antipsychotic drugs is Hermione Godswell. The drug they have got me on at the moment is called Aripiprazole. Its worst effect is to suppress my sexual feelings and it also makes my mouth and throat dry so my speech is slurred and my singing voice as well. I won't be doing any more concerts until I come off this horrible drug and get my normal voice back.

**Tuesday 12<sup>th</sup> July** 2016. Lucy and I made love again yesterday morning but this morning, Jasmin 2 prevailed in my thoughts. I danced with her and in my weakness I offered her the job of being my mistress. Those who have read *My Journey There* will know that Jasmin 2 was as near perfect a mistress as a man can have. I couldn't fault her in that role. No wonder I spent thirty-five years trying to get her back after she left me. She made a lousy wife but a perfect mistress. I don't really want a mistress. I want the love of a good wife who I will be a good husband to, and that woman is Lucy. I just hope I can be stronger in future when other women try to seduce me.

Maybe the ex-Prime Minister, Gordon Brown got it right when he repeatedly said, "We should all come together!" Maybe the solution is a mental communal orgasm, in which everyone who is 'in the know' comes together.

I heard a song a few days ago in which there was a line in the lyric which said that if you meet God just bow your head and call him Sir. Some of the people in this hospital, patients and staff, call me Sir. So there are people who know who I am. I just wish my responsible clinician, Marionette Madre, was one of them.

**Wednesday 13th July 2016**. I have been sleeping in my recliner chair every night since it arrived. It is a lot more comfy than my bed and it is therapeutically better for me. My legs are now feeling a lot better than before. I don't know if that is because of the recliner or the acupuncture, or both. I'll be visiting the acupuncturist again tomorrow and I'm looking forward to it. Doctor Madre hasn't spoken to me since I sent her the first page of this chapter, in which I accused one of her care team of having an ulterior motive for keeping me on these horrible drugs. They call jealousy the 'green-eyed god' and Hermione Godswell suffers badly from it.

One of the drawbacks of being an attractive man is that other women may be jealous of your chosen one!

If I understand it right, the solution found by the prophet Muhammed was to marry all of them. He ended up with four wives! I don't envy the chap, he had four mothers-in-law!

# Chapter 5
## Fear and Courage

**Friday 22ⁿᵈ July 2016**. I was due for my third acupuncture session yesterday but the staff here had not made an entry in the diary about it so it had to be cancelled and rebooked for next week.

Life is a bit humdrum at the moment. I still haven't heard from Lucy. I'm waiting for her to find the courage of an adult person. For a long time she has been living in fear of a man who is exploiting her. He controls her and tells her who she can and cannot communicate with. When she realises who she is she should have the courage to tell this man to go to hell. I think this man has been taking her money off her so she is living in poverty when, as a successful actress, she should be a wealthy woman by now.

When she finds the courage to stand up to this bully and tell him she is no longer afraid of him, he will then have no power over her at all.

If he does get violent, I'm sure Lucy knows some boys who will get him back, with interest! All she has to do is tell him that she will send the boys round to pay *him* a visit if he starts any nonsense.

I want to tell Lucy that there was a time in my life when I was living in fear but I realised that the solution to fear is not obedience, it is to have courage.

One of my major ambitions in life is to make Lucy happy. I am a firm believer in the saying that a happy wife makes for a happy life!

**Saturday 23ʳᵈ July 2016**. I sent Lucy a copy of the above entry, together with a covering letter, so she will know my current thoughts. I do hope she replies to my letters one day.

I've been writing to her since 1999. I've sent her poems and songs that I've written for her but she hasn't replied once. That is what makes me think that there is an evil man who is controlling her. I got the better of the Devil himself, when I though he was the one controlling Lucy, but whoever is controlling her had better learn from my track record that his days of bullying Lucy Lawless are numbered.

To change the subject, my acupuncture treatment is beginning to work. My legs are starting to get stronger, even though my buttocks hurt quite a lot still. It will be my third treatment on Thursday, so I'm looking forward to some more success.

I'm still waiting to hear from Olympia Publishers how well *My Journey There* is selling. They have said that we must be patient but they must also be keen to know the score. I do know that Waterstones in Glasgow have featured my book in a stand in a prominent place in their shop. So everybody in Glasgow knows where to buy my book if they want to. Some of my peers connected to this hospital have told me that they have purchased a copy.

There seems to be a growing movement of people wanting to 'close the door'. I have already explained in previous writing that this is a euphemism for getting rid of my late mother's soul, which is still causing mischief. I have given her until the end of this calendar year to start trying to get me the justice I seek or I will expel her from the human race. So far, all she does is to make the newscasters talk about people seriously ill in hospital, with the obvious implication that that is how people are to treat me.

I studied some 'care plan' documents yesterday and they were a load of insults against me wrapped up in psychobabble. This only makes me hate my mother even more. She has got an awful lot of back pedalling to do if she is to save her soul, but I will stick to my word and give her to the end of this year to start putting things right.

**Sunday 31st July 2016**. Everything is going smoothly. Contracts have been signed with Olympia Publishers for the publication of *My Journey Back – Part One*. So for some time I will be writing this book, *My Journey Back – Part Two*, whilst proofreading and sorting out *My Journey Back – Part One*.

I sensed that Lucy has received my correspondence concerning how to treat this evil man who has been controlling her. She knows that the world is watching to see how well she follows my advice. Everybody wants to know what she is made of.

I am considering going on a hunger strike until Doctor Madre and her team take me off the so-called antipsychotic medication. I think I will threaten to do so first and see what happens. I shall tell Daisy my current thinking on this subject. (You should recall that Daisy is the name of my primary nurse.) There is so much good food available that a hunger strike would be hard and an adult person has to eat to live. I want my sex drive back, so I've got to get off the medication. I can't think of a more appropriate way of twisting Marionette's arm than by not eating.

**Monday 1st August 2016**. I have not mentioned to anyone about my plan to go on a hunger strike and I have had a better idea. I think my original plan was best. That is to wait until Lucy makes her entrance on my social scene and then Lucy and I will close the door together.

I keep a light on in my room for Lucy 24/7.

I am confident that Lucy will be in touch with me soon and I am prepared to wait for her. I am also confident that when Lucy and I are a social item, and my mother's soul has been removed, then Doctor Marionette Madre and her team of care workers will take me off the accursed medication. It is because of my mother's influence mainly, that I have been on libido-suppressing drugs for almost all of the last forty years. She is still making sure that if she can't have me sexually, then no one else can. I had considered doing her a favour by dancing with her but I find it impossible to do that kind of a favour to someone I hate so much.

All my life, my mother's treatment of me has been inhuman, so I have no quibble about sending her down to be an animal in her next life.

**Tuesday 2nd August 2016.** I haven't done much today except trying to dance with Lucy and failing, the Aripiprazole; affects me so much that I can't even get an erection. The last time I saw Doctor Marionette Madre, I told her that I have realised that the suppression of my sex drive is the main effect that they are trying to achieve and not just an unfortunate side-effect. It is my jealous mother's influence, mainly, that I am treated this way. The only thing about me that makes the shrinks think I am mentally ill is that I refuse to have sex with my mother. I don't even like the woman, although millions of men all over the world still think of 'opening the door' as a ritual for graduating into manhood. This is still the case even though she has been dead for about ten years!

Doctor Marionette Madre asked one of our junior occupational therapists to ascertain what criteria we patients have to suggest in order to establish that we are no longer mentally ill. The old girl still has yet to prove herself. If she did, then she would know the criteria. It is supposed to be her forte as a consultant forensic psychiatrist to know whether a person is a real adult yet. But she doesn't even know that herself, so she cannot judge other people.

I have tried to tell her that a person is no longer a risk once they have found God. For I am the Lord God and there are millions of people in all walks of life, all over the world, that know this.

Whenever I come into the world as a human being, I am called upon to prove my Godhood. Last time I was here I sacrificed my beloved son, Jesus Christ, to prove my love for my people. I will say no more about this here, except to say that this time I have finally disposed of our main enemy, Satan, for ever. It may be conceivable that at some stage in the dim and distant future he may find a way to challenge me again, but for the foreseeable future he is nothing more than a rather nasty DOG and that is all he will be.

**Thursday 4<sup>th</sup> August 2016**. The newscasters on telly are now talking about people who have been discharged from hospitals, especially psychiatric hospitals. My efforts now seem to be getting some recognition and society is beginning to see things my way. The influence of my mad and decadent mother seems to be diminishing.

# Chapter 6
## Love

**Monday 8<sup>th</sup> August 2016.** I had a meeting on Friday with Doctor Madre and Daisy. I had previously given Daisy a copy of Chapter 5 of this book. Daisy told me she had read the copy and forwarded a copy to Doctor Madre. Based on what Daisy had told her, Doctor Madre has decided to seek the approval of her care team to give me a trial period without medication to see if I can get along without it OK. She is due to meet the care team on Wednesday of this week so, hopefully, I'll be coming of the accursed stuff this week.

I have still had no word from Lucy. The love I have for Lucy is, in the words of the anthem, *I Vow to Thee my Country*, a love that asks no questions, a love that stands the test, that lays upon the altar, the dearest and the best.

My father sacrificed his second wife, whom he loved dearly, to give the human race its best chance of survival against the hordes of Satan. Those hordes are now leaderless thanks mainly to myself, for trouncing the Devil and expelling him from the human race. We will, however, have to keep our guard up for they are bound to regroup under a new leader one day. When that happens, they will find that we are ready for them. I cannot see any serious threat to mankind from any beings in the foreseeable future.

**Friday 12<sup>th</sup> August 2016.** My late mother is still promoting her protégé, Rebecca, as the golden girl whom I must take for a wife. My mother and her protégé can go to hell as far as I'm concerned. Every time things look like going my way and the media start promoting my attitudes, my mother reasserts her influence, against the will of most people. Because of this I have decided that I am no longer bound by my promise to give her until the end of this year to start putting things right for me. The door must be closed as soon as possible.

I saw Doctor Madre again yesterday and she told me that next week there will be another visit from someone in my catchment area to interview me concerning a possible transfer to a hospital nearer my home district. Because of this, she is not going to take me off the Aripiprazole just yet as she does not want this doctor to see me whilst I am on a trial period without the medication.

I feel like someone who brings his own beer to a party and then is not allowed to drink; not even his own beer.

The whole adult world, especially Great Britain, is suffering from schizophrenia at the moment; my generation and Lucy's, want me at the top of the greasy pole by right of who I am and have proven myself to be. A dwindling band of supporters of my late mother still see her as the one who runs the show even though she has been dead for about ten years. I am sure that we will win, but I will need Lucy to help me close the door. Everyone is watching Lucy; to see what she is made of. Can she break free from whoever it is that's keeping her from me?

I am sending a copy of this chapter, this far, to Lucy, as she ought to know for sure what is going on where I live.

**Wednesday 17th August 2016**. I have been trying to speak to Doctor Madre since Friday of last week to ask her to take me off the Aripiprazole, visiting doctor notwithstanding. To further the metaphor about the beer at the party, this is exactly the kind of trick my mother would play on me. Knowingly or not, Dr Madre is complicit with my mother's wishes. I cannot see why I should be on an antipsychotic drug just because a visiting doctor is coming next week. Doctor Madre is aware that I have only been on these drugs for the last forty years because my jealous mother doesn't want me to have a sex life with any other woman than herself. She knows that I know this, so what has it got to do with a visiting doctor?

The heinous torture of being deprived of a sex life for forty years because of my mother's jealousy is one that the psychiatric community will have to answer to ME for in their next lives. I do not think I will be having much mercy on their souls.

I am sending a copy of this chapter, this far, to Doctor Madre today.

**Friday 19th August 2016**. Great Britain is doing so well at the Olympic Games, that a lot of other countries are asking the question, "What have they got that we haven't?" The answer of course is ME. The world must know that I really do exist and I am looking after the human race as I have always done.

British diplomats in all the corners of the Earth must have some missionary zeal about them. I repeat, I am the Lord God, by any name such as 'Allah' or whatever and this is *my* way of bringing peace to the world.

I don't know much about astrology but it seems to me that the world is now entering a new era. It is an era in which there is no Satan to give people the jitters and fear for the survival of our species. Perhaps it is the Age of Aquarius. It is an age in which harmony and understanding, sympathy and trust abound. I can't remember all the lyrics to the song, it comes from the musical, *Hair*, which came out in the 1960s. It is called *This is the Dawning of the Age of Aquarius*.

**Saturday 20th August 2016**. Many people make the tenuous connection of Aquarius, meaning, 'pertaining to water' and my family name of Brooks; a brook being a small stream of water. This then is the age in which I and my father before me, are heralding into the world.

This is my way of fulfilling the words of The Lord's Prayer, 'Thy Kingdom come, Thy will be done, on Earth as it is in Heaven... For Thine is the Kingdom, the power and the glory, for ever and ever. Amen'.

**Monday 22nd August 2016**. I am now sending a copy of this page to Doctor Madre. She has already received the first two pages of this chapter.

# Chapter 7
## Stalemate

**Thursday 25ᵗʰ August 2016**. I was due to see someone called Doctor Strange yesterday but she did not visit me, although she did visit this hospital and see some other patients. I was later told that she saw me in December of last year and did not need to see me again now. I had previously seen Doctor Madre who told me she would be keeping me on the medication as long as she is my doctor, whatever I decide about Doctor Strange's proposal.

You read in chapter 6 that this is my mother's sort of trick to play on me, like the beer at the party. reading between the lines of what Doctor Madre was saying, is that I have to get rid of my mother's soul from the spirit world or stay on the drugs. The only alternative is to become a necrophiliac motherfucker and concede that my mother is God, not me. This is a route that I refuse to go down. I would rather turn her into an animal and make her forfeit her humanity, which is no less than she deserves after the way she has treated me all my life. This is what is meant by 'closing the door'.

I still leave a light on in my room for Lucy 24/7.

I have arranged with my solicitor to have another mental health review tribunal hearing. This will take place on Monday 14ᵗʰ November this year so we have about two and a half months to get things sorted out. If Lucy enters my social scene before the tribunal hearing then I will stand a good chance of getting the absolute discharge that I am asking for. I have enough money to look after Lucy and myself for a while until I start getting revenue from the sales of my books. Of course I still have my state pension and I also will have the freedom to upload my music onto the Amazon website and also Apple i-tunes, so I can expect some income from my music as well. I have faith in my future and Lucy's if she agrees to become *my* partner.

It's all up to Lucy now. I need her to enter my life so we can finally close the door and be happy together. I am sending a copy of this chapter so far, of this book, to Lucy. I love Lucy and I want the world to know it.

**Friday 26th August 2016**. I love Lucy's sense of humour. I love the way she uses people without them realising it until her goal is achieved and then they can all share the joke. Her style really is delightful. People who play Lucy's game invariably get what they want out of life but people who seek to bully her or take advantage of her always end up regretting this attitude.

My attitude is simple. I love Lucy unconditionally. Whatever her behaviour, I love her beautiful soul. It complements mine perfectly. That's why I call her my soulmate. I know what I'm talking about.

**Sunday 28th August 2016**. I heard yesterday from the publishers that sales of *My Journey There* are not doing as well as we had hoped. In order to boost sales, the publishers got a professional book review made by Wordpress.com. The critic was very impressed by my book and gave it a splendid review and a four-star rating. I have also asked for book reviews from three people who I know have read the book and they have all agreed to give it a review for me. They are all professional men and will give an honest appraisal of the work. I am sure sales will be successful in the long run but it is not the kind of book that becomes an immediate bestseller overnight; news of the book will filter down by word of mouth and by good reviews and good publicity, all of which will happen.

Doctor Madre uses the promise of a drug free trial and the continuation of the drug as a carrot and a stick with which to get me to do her bidding. I think Doctor Madre wants me to close the door and is not frank enough to tell me so, so she uses the threat of the drug to make me do what she wants, once I have guessed correctly what that is. I think my mother's soul is doomed now, whatever attitude she takes to anything or anyone. People like Doctor Madre are making sure of it.

One thing I know for sure is that once the door has been closed, no one except an idiot will dare to tell me what to do again, because I will then be the undisputed King. I expect that there will always be idiots who think they can manipulate me and those whose motives are bad will get the chop.

All I can do now is wait until I hear from Lucy. She has GOT TO FIND A WAY TO ENTER MY LIFE SOMEHOW. I accidently hit the caps lock when typing the above sentence. I was going to correct it but then I thought it was meant to be that way. I'm sending her this page as well. The ball is in her court and if she doesn't knock it back then I will assume she doesn't want to play with me. I don't think I will be writing to Lucy any more after this letter. If she doesn't reply, then I will assume Aphrodite got it wrong when she made me think my destiny was to be with Lucy. I will just stay single and assume that the human race has let me down when it promised me the woman of my choice.

**Wednesday 31st August 2016**. Yesterday morning, I refused to take the Aripiprazole tablet that these people want me to take. The stuff has several horrible side effects, as well as what I think is the main effect and the real purpose of the drug, which is to totally suppress my sexual functioning. Doctor Madre denies that this is the main purpose of the drug but I don't believe her and I told her so. I expected the staff to report this to Doctor Madre and for her to pay me a visit to try and make me take the drug but unbeknown to me, Doctor Madre is away on annual leave all this week and next week. I had been anticipating a showdown with her and to assert my authority as the King to put her in her place but instead, I was given a visit by Doctor Cowslip who is acting as the responsible clinician in Doctor Madre's absence.

Doctor Cowslip took over from Doctor Dilly Buttercup, who I wrote about previously. Doctor Buttercup retired a little while ago. I had known Doctor Cowslip from when I was on Northgate ward. She seems much more reasonable to me now than she was then. I reminded Doctor Cowslip that Doctor Madre had promised me a drug free trial period before Doctor Strange's visit and that Doctor Madre had changed her mind subsequently, as I may have wanted to go to another hospital of Doctor Strange's choice. I pointed out to Doctor Cowslip that not only had Doctor Strange not visited me when she came here recently but whatever Doctor Strange said, I did not want to leave Alcatraz Island Hospital as long as I was not on any so-called antipsychotic drugs.

Doctor Cowslip did not put up a strong case for me to be on the drug, so I won the day yesterday and I am now on a drug free trial period.

Yesterday I experienced quite bad withdrawal symptoms but it was nothing I couldn't handle; in fact, I was quite relieved because this bodes well for the rest of the trial period. I'm already starting to feel more like my old self again and although I haven't had any sexual experiences without the drug yet, I've got good reason to hope that I'll soon be dancing with Lucy again and I'm looking forward to enjoying some beer at the party.

Nobody knows how long this trial period will last for. I assume it will last for the rest of my life. I don't ever want to go back to being on neuroleptic drugs again. I am as happy as I want to be in Alcatraz Island hospital off the drugs. Of course I would rather be free but I think that while I am waiting for Lucy, Alcatraz Island is as good a place as any to pass the time. It is a cloud with a very good silver lining because it doesn't cost me much to be here and I get to save most of my pension each week. When I get my discharge, I will be glad of the money I've managed to save. Although I sleep alone, I have my own room here and there is always plenty of company for me to enjoy so I am never lonely. Not that I mind my own company anyway. It is always interesting to hear other people's stories.

Concerning my mother's fate, a lot of people say things thinking I will draw the wrong conclusions from them and blame my mother, whose influence is now very limited. Some people say that compassion is not a weakness but a strength. Other people call me a prince and not a king for having compassion on my mother. To be perfectly frank, I don't care anymore about her fate. She made me prove that I outrank her and she and all her followers have to accept that fact. As long as she doesn't interfere with my love life, especially with Lucy, then I will leave her alone and trust that she does the same for me. There is evidence to imply that she is trying to get me the four things I want by way of justice from British society, which was what I asked of her, so I will wash my hands of any plans to upset her. She has had her day and everybody knows it.

It is nearly eight now in the evening and I will be going to bed soon. Before I retire to bed though, I just want to record that my sex life is back to its best. I danced with someone (I don't know who, for sure) this afternoon and reached a sexual climax. Prior to this afternoon, I hadn't had an orgasm for weeks but with just two drug-free mornings to go on, I am back on form and I am well pleased with the situation.

**Thursday 1st September 2016.** It's just gone five in the morning and I want to put it on record that I feel great. All my nerves are rejoicing with a good feeling now that I am free from neuroleptic drugs. That is not all. I can feel Lucy's love for me. I don't know what is keeping her from me but whatever it is, it is not as strong as our love for each other, so I'm sure she will get in touch with me soon. My feelings for Lucy are stronger than the forces of life and death, and I can feel that Lucy feels the same way about me. I wish to quote to the reader of this narrative a verse from a poem I wrote for Lucy sixteen years ago:

Whoever comes between us,

Whoever even tries,
Will curse their luck forever
With no soul to hear their cries.
For we no longer are constrained,
We live in Paradise regained,
The serpent's gone and we now reign
Wherever there are skies.

The only thing that has changed in those sixteen years is that we have now proven what I wrote then.

To change the subject, I received a review of my book, *My Journey There*, yesterday, from one of my fellow patients, a friend of mine called Neil Gooding. Neil is a professional poet and is a man who was educated at Oxford University. He speaks with an Oxford accent which sometimes surprises people as he is a black-skinned man. I thought you might like to read Neil's review, so I'm quoting it here:

## Neil Gooding's Review

### A Review of Robert Brooks Strong's Book My Journey There
### By published poet Neil Gooding
### (AKA L.S. Kimberley)
### Trinidadian Poet

This book is a revelation. It reveals hidden truths. Robert Strong is not out of his depth when coming to write anything about his life and others. He has, of course, his own views on life and does not force you to believe them. His style is very literary and not too self-conscious. Since we are reading something of someone's life story, it is necessary that we get a picture of the events as they unfold. The stories in Robert Strong's book rapidly unfold to give a picture – sometimes of desperation, sometimes of unsurety – hooked with strong convictions. Robert might write 'The relationship between Father Time and Mother Nature is a permanent battle to see who wears the pants in their household'. The personification of Time and Nature adds to this angst-driven book. Since Robert Brooks is literary, he is also versed in the ways of what 'good literature' is. He was a competent computer expert. He is knowledgeable, time and again about morality, though he sometimes may be on the wrong fence of it. All in all, Robert Strong is a strong, genuine writer. He has a genius for the discursive. There is nothing petty about him.

I hope that those of you who have read *My Journey There* will agree with Neil.

I have just come back from an interview with a shrink called Doctor Mouse who is my responsible clinician whilst Doctor Madre is away on holiday. He has decided to put me back on the Aripiprazole because he hasn't got the guts to let me have my own way on the subject of the medication. I have just been given by Daisy an Aripiprazole tablet so it looks like I am not going to enjoy my beer after all.

Mouse made the point that Marionette Madre will be back from holiday in eleven days' time, so maybe she will take me off the drug, but he hasn't got the guts to do so, especially as he is only acting temporarily in my case.

I will just have to be patient a little longer for an appointment with Marionette Madre. I told Mouse that he is a coward and that I would sooner be myself than him. I also told him that the shrinks all swear by the medication although none of them have ever taken the stuff themselves, so their attitude is the sick one, not mine. They have faith in the stuff like some crazy religious cult. Although none of them know what they are talking about from first-hand experience.

All the shrinks are using the drugs as a stick to beat me with until I take their attitude to my mother. There is a body of opinion in this country, and the world, that wants ME to close the door and the shrinks are spearheading this movement. No matter how merciful I prove myself to be, the shrinks want me to bring Dolly (my mother) back as an animal. Under the circumstances, I am going to fall in line with this body of opinion. I feel a bit like King James after signing the Magna Carta. The barons got their own way. Now the latter-day barons are the shrinks and they want me to have the removal of my mother from the human race on my conscience. Knowing that the same thing might happen to me in a few short years' time. I shall just have to play my cards more wisely than my mother did.

I think I will need help; hopefully I'll get it from Lucy as well as everyone else who wants me to close the door. I want the door closed as soon as possible; this must happen soon. I have set a target date OF THE END OF NEXT WEEK. (Again, I'm letting the capital letters ride), when Marionette Madre comes back from holiday. The only thought I have now is HOW?

**Friday 2<sup>nd</sup> September 2016**. The newscasters on the telly are still encouraging people to open the door, so there is now open warfare between those who want to see the end of Dolly's reign and those who want to deify her and keep her cult alive forever as a new religion.

I am caught in the crossfire between these opposing attitudes. I stated my view earlier in this chapter but the shrinks hold the trump card of the neuroleptic drugs. They not only want the door closed but they insist that it is me who closes it. I do not know if the water fowl are still enjoying their mating season at the moment, but I do know that rats mate all the year round, so I am going to turn Dolly into a rat. If she would rather be a duck or a goose then she can try to catch a copulating drake or gander and come back to life herself as one such creature, if, that is, the water fowl are still mating at this time of year.

**Thursday 8th September 2016.** This is just a line to say that nothing happened on Sunday. I think we will have to wait until Lucy comes to visit me before we are able to close the door.

**Wednesday 14th September 2016.** Life still goes on whilst I am waiting for Lucy. I went to Brixton and North Hampshire Hospital yesterday for a consultation about my prostate gland. The alternative is to carry on using catheters for the rest of my life. At the moment I cannot urinate naturally and I have to use a catheter to empty my bladder, which I do three times a day.

Under the circumstances, I told the consultant that I wish to have the operation. He told me that he would put me on the waiting list for the operation and it would take two or three months before we have the operation. In any event, he said to me, we should get it done before Christmas. It will mean a stay of one or two nights in hospital but I don't mind that. I am therefore, looking forward to getting my waterworks sorted out before Christmas. Even if I am one of the forty per cent on whom the operation doesn't work, I will be no worse off than I am now.

**Friday 16th September 2016.** I have just had a long and exhausting interview with a very nice chap called Doctor White. He was commissioned by my solicitor as an independent psychiatrist for my forthcoming tribunal hearing. The interview lasted an hour and a half, and I told him most of the salient points about my life history. I am wondering what kind of report he will produce and I am looking forward to it.

I went to the acupuncturist again yesterday afternoon, and I told him truthfully that my legs, hips and back felt a lot better than they have done of late. What I didn't tell him was that I have recently embarked upon a course of treatment known as Detox Foot Patches. They remove all the odious toxins from the body while you sleep. I am starting to feel much better already. I have also discovered a treatment known as acupressure insoles. I have been wearing these for a few days now and at first they made my legs feel tired, but once I got used to them they have helped me to feel good about all sorts of aches and pains which were worrying me. I have joined the ranks of old people who are trying to keep their age from stopping them enjoying life; we just like to give the grim reaper a run for his money, even though we all know he will win in the end!

**Sunday 18th September 2016**. It is shortly after 12 a.m. and I can't get any sleep so I thought I'd get my thoughts down in writing while they are still in my mind.

Yesterday had the auspicious date, the seventeenth. There was an uncanny stillness in the air yesterday which made me think something was happening or about to happen. Consequently, I tried as hard as I could to ratify my mother's soul. I can turn any ordinary soul into a rat but with the gods, it is much harder and needs the full support of the human race. I am now getting this support, just like I did when I dogified Satan.

I get a feeling that I know what is going on in my mother's mind. She doesn't know *what* she is anymore. She is changing into a rat and I think we are at last closing the door. If I am wrong and she finds a way to escape this fate, on this occasion, then we will keep on trying until we do succeed in closing the door. With the support I now command, we shouldn't have much difficulty.

**Monday 19th September** 2016. It is now twenty past five in the morning and I have been watching the news on the telly. One of the women on the box was saying something about some business deal or other and in the conversation she said the deal had not yet been ratified. The use of this keyword tells me that Dolly's soul has not yet been irreversibly turned into the body of a rat. The whole ethos of the media and that of ordinary men and women I hear talking, is that my mother has now had her day and everybody knows it.

Even Dolly herself knows that she has got to go now, so I am now telling the world to keep up the pressure on her, full time, until she is finally ratified. I think it will happen today, which, coincidentally, is my eldest son, Anthony's birthday. He is fifty-one today and I want to say that the ratification of my mother is the best possible birthday present we can give to him and his generation.

**Friday 23<sup>rd</sup> September 2016**. I heard on the television news this morning, American Secretary of State for Foreign Affairs, James Kerry, (I think that's his name) saying that the peace talks with the Russians about the war in Syria had broken down because he is finding it increasingly hard to keep the door open. This tells me that it is not just here in Great Britain that the civil war between my mother's army and mine is being waged, but it is now a battle for the leadership of the worlds; both temporal and spiritual.

It is taking longer than I thought it would, but the stalemate is now drawing to a conclusion, as is this chapter of *My Journey Back – Part Two*.

# Chapter 8
## Goodbye Dolly

I can think of several things I want to say to Lucy and also things to say to my shrink, Doctor Marionette Madre. These things will not be said though until I meet with each person and have the opportunity to say them face to face.

Dolly, (my mother) knew many years ago that this day would come. She realised years ago that the world is not big enough for me, my wife and herself. She therefore made a decision to enjoy herself as much as she could at my expense and that of Lucy and all of the other girlfriends I have had in my life. Every girl I have ever been serious about has turned into a woman of easy virtue (in other words a SLUT). There goes that caps lock key again! I realised that this was the pattern of my relationships many years ago and I thought that was just human nature. What I didn't realise was that there was a mind and the will of an evil person behind this pattern of behaviour and that person was my mother. She would do anything to destroy my relationships with any woman other than herself! There were no exceptions to this rule, not even girls whom she approved of and were sycophantic towards her.

I am the Lord God and you can thank *me* for the taboo against incest. Were it not for that taboo, the human race would degenerate into a weak and stupid species who would no longer be in control of the world and our place as the dominant life form would no longer apply. That is what our enemies hoped for when they sent their leader, Satan, into the world in human form. Luckily for mankind, I proved stronger than him and my heart and mind are in the right place.

Dolly hoped to turn me into her toy boy and to make a motherfucker out of me. My dad's second wife, Iris, had the same notion. Needless to say, neither of these two dragons stood any chance at all of making their perverted dreams come true.

Now that Dolly has tried and failed to stop me from loving Lucy, her whole interest in humanity has evaporated. She knows that she is destined to be a rat in her next life and I think I have even made her look forward to her next life as a creature who can perform incest and not worry about it. I don't think rats share our taboos, which should suit my mother and her followers. They will all be ratified along with her.

She is a woman at the edge of a precipice and she lacks the courage to jump, so we will have to push her.

I want Lucy to realise that that is her job as the new first lady of society. Just like the bees, the newly emerging queen has to finish off the old queen who has served her purpose. Unlike the bees, we have a king as well as a queen. Perhaps there can only be one real monarch, in which case maybe I shall have to push Dolly myself, although I proved I'm the new monarch when I killed Iris forty years ago. I still say it is Lucy's job to turn Dolly into a rat because I want her to do something to prove she is worthy to be my wife. No man-made law can touch a person for their behaviour in the spirit world.

It suits Dolly to feel that she is sacrificing her own humanity so that we may live and enjoy ours. If I thought there was anything human left in her now, I would thank her. As it is, I am saying, "Thank for nothing. Now get out, whatever you are."

I want to say this to everybody, that if we all say this loud enough and say it now, she will have to go. So, tell her, everybody, loud and clear. Tell her to get out. Now! Goodbye and good riddance, you evil, incestuous old witch.

# Chapter 9
## The Queen is The Queen?

**Wednesday 28<sup>th</sup> September 2016**. I was called in to see the members of the Multi-Disciplinary Team (AKA the MDT) this morning. Doctor Madre tried to tell me that the drug she is currently forcing me to take is not the cause of my sexual malfunctioning. She tried to blind me with science by talking about the various chemicals that were part of the drug. I simply pointed out that I recently went for two days without the drug and achieved two orgasms in that time when it has been several weeks since I had an orgasm when I have been taking the tablets, so I still don't believe her.

She is changing my medication to one called Risperidone which I can also have in tablet form. At least I won't have any more injections.

I confess I let my exasperation show when I said to her and all the team, "What do you people want from me?" It seems to me that it is society that is mentally ill, not me, when the only use to which it can put a many-skilled man like me, is to be a human guinea pig for the psychiatrists' drugs. I began to fear that I am destined to spend the rest of my life in psychiatric care and on neuroleptic drugs. Doctor Madre said that she was treating me this way to treat my mental illness! Something I have always denied I suffer from. I have never felt ill in that way. "What then," I asked myself, "is the real reason I have been treated this way for forty years?"

For a long time I blamed my late mother's influence but she has been dead for about ten years now and her influence is a lot weaker now than it was when she was alive. Who then do the shrinks look to for leadership and purpose in their behaviour?

Then it dawned on me.

The penny dropped, so to speak.

I have been trying to make a queen out of Lucy, when this country has a perfectly good queen already. Once can debate people's personal qualities until one is blue in the face but no one can deny that Her Majesty Queen Elizabeth II is not only the queen but a very popular queen, to many people all over the world. The mystery that has been puzzling me was that the queen has been playing 'hide and seek' with me. She is the person with the highest profile in the world, arguably, yet she maintains a low profile for fun!

I think the queen must love me. That doesn't surprise me after all I've done for humanity; and her role is a leading ONE IN HUMANITY. (There goes that caps lock button again.) And I love her as my monarch, although I still love Lucy as my sweetheart and the one I want for my wife. For obvious reasons a personal relationship between the queen and me is out of the question, so I don't think about it.

In many ways I am lucky. In olden days I would have been killed for saying the things I have said. Nowadays the shrinks exist and enjoy royal approval for affording asylum to folk who are worth saving and educating. Even though, in some cases, it involves a lot of guessing games. Games which I, personally, am fed up with playing.

When foster parents look after a child, they are said to be in *loco parentis*, I am coining a new phrase by saying that my mother was acting in *loco regentis*. In other words, as a substitute monarch. Dolly and Elizabeth never met but they both agreed who was whom. Dolly's fate is still in the balance but it doesn't worry me anymore. There are signs that she is trying to get me the four things I want by way of justice for myself. So I'm not going to upset myself by trying to do anything to her; she'll do that for herself.

**Thursday 29ᵗʰ September 2016.** The thought that Elizabeth is the source of my misfortune was just a red herring. The queen is not The Queen, Dolly is, even though she has been dead for about ten years. She has been playing God whilst I am still alive and live in the land of the living, unlike her. There is now no doubt in my mind. I have got to get rid of my mother – I have no choice. Perhaps there is a place where geese are bred and mate all the year round by keeping the ganders in an artificially warm environment. I think this is likely. There is a pantomime called *Mother Goose* and I think this title is a reflection of my mother's destiny. I don't think the world is so cruel it will make me wait until next spring to get rid of her.

**Friday 30ᵗʰ September 2016**. Bernard Matthews has a turkey farm in Norfolk, so I don't see why someone shouldn't have a goose farm somewhere in the country. I am going to use my mind to find a gander and a female goose who are copulating. If I can find such a couple, I will stuff my mother's soul down into the gander's sperm cell and Bob's your uncle!

I do wish I had Lucy to help me. Dolly is the source of all Lucy's misfortunes and the one who has been pulling the strings of all the people who have abused her, so no one could blame Lucy for Dolly's eventual fate as Mother Goose. Dolly has only herself to blame. She used every dirty trick in the book, and some that aren't, in order to get me to have sex with her. Dolly was a Black Magic woman and she used the Devil himself to get me together with her.

Unfortunately for her, and all the other Black Magic practitioners, I proved stronger than the Devil, so *their* plans have all come to naught, just as they hoped mine would, and did when I was a boy. The only shelter that Satan can offer them now is for them to become animals in their next lives, for that is the hell that unrepentant sinners have to look forward to.

I have worked out why the shrinks say I suffer from mental illness. Mental illness is defined as, "Having thoughts which differ from those of Mrs Dorothy Ayres," and a mentally ill person is one who gives voice to such thoughts. Under those definitions I agree that I suffer from mental illness, but I won't for long.

My primary nurse, Daisy, said to me on one occasion, "You're the King, Bob." Many people have said that to me in my lifetime and I have believed them, because I wanted to, but they were all wrong. I am not the King, YET. I will be the king, however, when my mother's soul loses its identity and she becomes a gosling. THEN it will be the time to say, "The King is dead – Long live the King."

This will happen in the immediate future.

When I become King, I will obviously start by flexing my muscles, so to speak; to find out the extent and nature of my new powers. For example, I may go along with the mental illness model and keep everything the same except for the name of the person in charge. I may though, be so angry with the psychiatric profession that I decide to do away with psychiatry altogether and restore power to the religious fraternity. If I keep psychiatry, it will only be because of the motto of the Royal College of Psychiatrists, 'LET WISDOM PREVAIL'. (I put the caps lock on deliberately for that bit.)

I will also be changing the laws on same-sex relationships. Same-sex marriage disgusts me. To put sodomy on the same footing as love making between husband and wife is not even amusing. It makes a mockery of an institution which makes humans better than animals. I will also reinstate the meaning of the word 'gay'. Gay means happy, cheerful and light-hearted. It does not mean homosexual, nor lesbian. In fact, all the queers I know, and know of, are miserable characters and are not gay at all.

# Chapter 10
# Further Thoughts on the Future

**Tuesday 4<sup>th</sup> October 2016.** I sent copies of chapter 9 of this book to Doctor Marionette Madre and Lucy Lawless, with covering letters, on Friday of last week. Daisy was off work since Thursday and has only returned today, so I have now made a copy for her. I am wondering what effect they will have. I am hoping that Lucy is able to break free soon and Marionette backs me at my forthcoming tribunal hearing. I think they are both afraid of stepping outside of their 'comfort zone' because it seems as if this stalemate will go on forever.

I have a little involvement with the computer on this ward. I looked up 'Goose Farms in England' and there were many entries so I am sure to find a copulating gander and hen-goose to be Dolly's new parents. The hen is already famous. She is known as 'The goose that laid a golden egg'. That is what Dolly will be – 'the golden egg'.

I have a mental health review tribunal hearing next month, but I have asked my solicitor to try and postpone it to a date shortly before Christmas. This is because I am due for an operation on my prostate gland soon. The consultant at the hospital said it will happen before Christmas this year but he couldn't give me a definite date. I want to be in good health before I go to the tribunal.

If Lucy and I get together before the tribunal, then I think I will get an absolute discharge, in which case we will need a home to go to. I have been looking up on the internet for properties in what used to be coal mining communities. My circumstances are unusual so I have decided to write to estate agents in these districts explaining my circumstances and looking for a property under about £25,000. I can pay for such a property. I don't need a mortgage.

**Thursday 6<sup>th</sup> October 2016**. I can feel Lucy's love for me and it makes me very happy, even though the drugs which I am forced to take prohibit any sexual functioning. I think Lucy has received my letter which I enclosed with chapter 9 to her. This makes me think that I have hit the nail on the head with respects to this man. I think that he is the idiot controlling Lucy, because I mentioned him in my letter and today I can feel Lucy's love so very strongly. I am now going to print for you my letter to Lucy that I wrote last week.

Dear Lucy,

Please find enclosed a letter from myself to an estate agent. Please also find a copy of chapter 9 of *My Journey Back – Part two*.

I thought you would like to know my current thinking and behaviour. I am anticipating an absolute discharge on November 14<sup>th</sup>. It would be nice if we could get together before then. The man who calls himself 'The Main Man', has become the main figure of international ridicule. He is the one at the head of the extortion racket and the prostitution racket. You and all your friends will soon be free of him and his supporters.

Yours with love and friendship,

Bob Brooks Strong.

I wrote the above letter before I wrote to my solicitor asking her to postpone the tribunal hearing. It has always seemed to me that Lucy is basically A VERY FINE PERSON (There goes that caps lock button again!) and that the bad behaviour that she has committed in the past was a result of the abuse that she has had to suffer. I think she will soon be free of her evil controller and that as soon as she is able to, she will be here with me. After watching Lucy perform as Xena, I felt that she was a very fine person but now that we are together in spirit I know that she is the most wonderful woman in the world, she is Mother nature herself.

**Sunday 9th October 2016**. Lucy's spirit visited me this morning and we made love as only a man and a woman who really love each other can do. I never knew such happiness existed. We came together in spite of the fact that the drug I am forced to take suppresses my sex drive. True love conquers all! And who said that love is only for the young? Young love is blind but when you have found your soulmate then you can see everything.

I heard yesterday from my solicitor. The shrink she asked to do a report on me came up with a load of psychobabble and said that he would not recommend me for discharge, I don't think she received my letter asking for the tribunal to be postponed, so I wrote back enclosing a copy of the former letter asking for a postponement.

Lucy and I, and all our friends, are waiting for her evil controller to lose control of his vice networks. I think he is going to die soon because that's what a little dicky bird whispered in my ear! We are also waiting for my late mother, Dolly, to disappear into the world of geese. I'm sure that she will soon be saying 'Goodbye cruel world'. And I will reply, "And good riddance. You've had a good innings, now GO!"

I'm hoping that both of these events happen before my tribunal hearing. Hopefully that man will try to atone for his sins by giving Lucy back some of the money that he has extorted from her over the years. If that bastard wants to avoid being turned into a lobster in his next life, then he has got a lot to do to achieve salvation. I wouldn't need any prompting to turn him into a lobster, then arrange for him to be caught and boiled live to make a lobster thermidor for someone to eat. It is worth a mention that it is currently the mating season for marine crustaceans in the northern hemisphere.

My code word is 'CARA', which stands for Confess, Apologise, Repent and Atone. These are the things that a sinner must do to avoid being turned into some horrible creature. This is the only way to avoid having to forfeit one's humanity. This is what I mean by 'Salvation'. Those who don't achieve salvation are the unrepentant sinners who will go to hell. Some people may be controlled by that man's code word but whatever it is, CARA trumps it!

**Thursday 13th October 2016**. I had a visit yesterday from my solicitor, Ms Jane Rabbit. She had received my letters but she advised me that it is not realistic to postpone the tribunal hearing to an unspecified date in the future. She advised me that under the circumstances, it would be best if we withdraw the application for a tribunal hearing and then reapply after my operation. I accepted this advice and asked her to cancel the tribunal application.

It is going to cost me more than I can afford to buy a house. Even in the ex-coal mining communities, property is out of my reach. Not only that, but all property worth buying is sold by auction these days and I would have to be a free man to attend an auction.

**Saturday 15th October 2016**. For the last week or so, I have had a double dose of Risperidone every morning and just one tablet in the evening. It is now 3.49 pm and I have been trying all day to dance with Lucy, but the effect of the drug is too strong. I can't even get an erection. The psychiatric profession will regret treating *me* this way when I come to power. This will be when my late mother's soul loses its identity, which won't be long now. I repeat, the motto of the Royal College of Psychiatrists is 'Let Wisdom Prevail'. This has not been happening. Wisdom has not been prevailing. The neuroleptic drugs that I have had to take might have been useful a long time ago but it is not wise to make me take them the way things are at the moment.

I get the impression that Dolly has chosen to come back as a duck. There are many signs pointing to this conclusion, including the fact that her husband used to call her 'duck' as a term of endearment. He called her that for many years when they were both alive. I think they must both have known the future. I want everyone who knows how inhuman she has been to me (and my father and brother) to shout at her, "Good riddance to bad rubbish. Get out." I want to say to her, "You deserted us in 1951 because of your sexual desire for Maurice Ayres. Now the past has caught up with you! Get out, and take your decadent, incestuous desires with you."

This may seem like a bit of a rant to many people, but how am I supposed to feel when I have spent over forty years of my life in psychiatric hospitals? Most of those years in top security places, namely Broadmoor and Ashworth, all because I refused to have sex with my mother; the woman whose colloquial epithet is, *She who must be obeyed*. It was *her* influence in society that was the main cause of me being driven to homicide, when I killed Iris in 1976.

It was also Dolly who made use of the Devil himself to split up my relationship with Jasmin 2. An attempt which succeeded. When Satan took possession of Jasmin 2's mind on that island in Derwentwater in April 1970, he was obeying Dolly's wishes. It was Dolly's decadent, incestuous desire that caused me so much misery all my life. If she thinks I am going to repay her in the way she wants, she can think again. The longer she prolongs this agony, the longer it will be before I let her live as a human being again.

# Chapter 11
## Goodbye Dolly – 2

**Friday 21<sup>st</sup> October 2016**. My late mother, Dolly to most people, is still prolonging the agony of her existence and mine. Three alternatives have been mooted for her, a duck, a goose or a rat. I think she has chosen to become a duck, but that is something I don't mind. I just want her to get on with it. Perhaps she is enjoying being a disembodied spirit and playing God in the spirit world but I think not. I think she is still clinging to the hope that I will have mental sex with her. She still tries to interfere when I manage to get a dance with Lucy. Now Lucy has a personal motive for getting rid of Dolly, as well as a social obligation to do so.

It is Dolly's fault that I am still on neuroleptic drugs after forty years of having my body abused by these things. And some people still wonder why I hate my mother so much. I felt today that Lucy and I were dancing well and I was looking forward to giving and receiving sexual fulfilment with Lucy, when I felt my mother's spirit trying to muscle in on our enjoyment. I just froze. I hated her for spoiling Lucy's pleasure even more than my own. There is no way that I will ever give sexual pleasure to my mother, even though every other man in the world looks to her for sexual pleasure. She waS THE Global Village bike when she was alive and she still is, even though she has been dead for about ten years. (That caps lock button keeps working its magic.)

Perhaps after this exposition, she will get the message and go. I certainly hope so. When Dolly goes, she will take with her the epithet, '*She who must be obeyed*'. I think that most people will choose me as her successor but I am not taking that for granted. My people and I have many battles ahead of us but we will face the future with courage and wisdom and a sense of humour and when I die I hope people will say of me, "He left the world a better place than the one he found."

**Thursday 25ᵗʰ October 2016**. Yesterday I was feeling a little downhearted because I had not felt Lucy's spirit for a while, but then I had the most wonderful experience. I felt my mother and Lucy were fighting over me, with their mind and spirit. It was one hell of a fight and it isn't over yet. Both women are giving it their all and no one is giving the other any quarter. The outcome of this fight is something I am aware of because Aphrodite made me aware that my destiny is to settle down with Lucy. It feels so wonderful to know that Lucy knows I am worth fighting for. I think the fight will be over today. Earlier this morning, I looked up 'Duck Farms in England' on the computer and discovered that there are plenty of them. For a little while I thought that Dolly was getting the better of Lucy, so I gave Lucy all the encouragement I could and demanded that all Lucy's followers and all my supporters should give Lucy all the courage and all the strength to get her second wind and come back out fighting.

I have a saying that you can always squeeze an extra drop out of an empty bottle. This may seem impossible and logically it is of course. But how empty does a bottle have to be to deny my saying? What most people call empty is the exception that proves the rule of my saying.

It worked. Those who were pessimistic about Lucy's chance of beating Dolly have now got egg on their faces. Lucy is still fighting and the honours are about even. I am reminded of the words that heralded the opening of *Xena Warrior Princess*. The words are, 'Her courage will change the world'. I thought then, and still do, that although the words were ostensibly about Xena, they were also a portent of what was to come in the life of Lucy Lawless! The events of the morning prove me right. By typing today's entry in this book, I have weakened Dolly's resolve to fight much more. She knows now that she is losing. My job now is to find a randy drake and stuff

Dolly's soul into one of his sperm cells. Then Bob's your uncle and Lucy's your aunt. <u>Not</u> Fanny. This change in the old saying is my doing. I should remake the point that 'Fanny' is one of my father's names for my mother.

**Wednesday 26<sup>th</sup> October 2016**. Dolly won the fight that took place yesterday. But as the fight was over my heart and mind, then Lucy won it. Lucy and I were chewing over some consoling thoughts this morning and the biggest of these was that that fight, whoever won, has brought us together in spirit, even closer than before, (as if that were possible). The drug that they have got me on is very strong and I can't achieve a sexual climax on it. I was called to a meeting this morning with Doctor Madre and Daisy and two other women. Madre won't even give me a drug free trial period, let alone take me off the poisonous stuff. I am sure that my late mother is to blame for this, but it does no good explaining things to Doctor Madre.

For months now, I have been letting Doctor Madre and Daisy know my thoughts by giving them copies of the pages from this manuscript. This has been a waste of time while Dolly exists, even in spirit form. I have decided that nothing else matters in my life except making an animal out of my late mother's soul. Whilst her soul has her identity then the world is one big conspiracy to make me have sex with her. I may send Lucy the occasional letter but these psychiatric creeps are getting no more free information from me. I have nothing more to say to anyone now except, "Goodbye Dolly."

**Saturday 29<sup>th</sup> October 2016**. The fact that Dolly and Lucy were fighting has caused a lot of consternation among many members of society. Win or lose, both women have gained in reputation by being fighters.

I am so very proud of Lucy. I hope that she will soon be free of this creep who controls her. He seems to have a kind of spell on her, which some people call a 'code'. It seems to be some kind of hypnotic trance THAT SHE IS IN WHICH CONTROLS HER BEHAVIOUR. (The caps lock button seems to have a mind of its own.) I can help her break this spell. What she has to do is to identify the plausible lie that is the foundation stone of the belief system. When the key premise is identified to be the lie which the rest of the thoughts and ideas depend on, then she will be able to kick this control freak (for that is what he is) out of her mind.

I feel sure that Lucy will soon be free to contact me, when she can say and do what she wants.

A clever hypnotist will even get his subject to forget the false premise that was the start of the belief system, so that the subject will not even know *why they cannot do or say what they want to*. (This time it was the italics button which seemed to have a mind of its own.) What Lucy must do now is to <u>remember</u> the things that this man said when she first had contact with him, for therein lies the answer to the puzzle that has been confusing her.

I am fighting this man and Lucy's mind is the battlefield.

Lucy is not a fool. I think she understands what I have been telling her, and victory is close at hand now for Lucy and therefore for me.

My late mother, Dolly, has been saying her last goodbyes to the people she knows, for she will be departing soon. Everybody knows that there is no longer a place for her in human society. That is just one of the hard facts of life that we all have to accept. All good things must come to an end.

I do not intend to finish this chapter until I am sure Dolly is gone.

I wrote to three estate agents about houses for sale and none of them have replied. I have decided to consider property in Scotland. I think there may well be parts of rural Scotland where I can find a house in my price range. There are many signs that Scotland may well be the place for me and Lucy. Such as Doctor Watson's saying 'Great Scot, Holmes!' and the saying 'Scot free' and 'The Flying Scotsman'.

I will get back on the computer ASAP to look up property in Scotland. I am optimistic of finding somewhere good in Scotland.

Doctor Madre starts another two-week holiday on Monday, so there is no chance of coming off the drug which is chemically castrating me before then. So Lucy and I must remain patient and suffer for a bit longer.

To clarify my position in respect to my succession, Lucy will be my Queen consort and when I die, she will be the Queen regent. When Lucy dies, Troy will be THE King and his wife will be Queen consort. That is my will.

**Thursday 3rd November 2016**. Last time I wrote to Lucy I mentioned the probability of us living in Scotland. One of the signs for this is the name of the steam train, 'The Flying Scotsman'. This locomotive has a companion steam train called 'The Mallard'. A mallard is a wild duck!

**Friday 4th November 2016**. I'm still not sure that Dolly has gone yet. When I am sure, it will be the end of this chapter and the end of an era in human affairs. Now that I have got the joke about the eider and the joke about the mallard, there is nothing left for Dolly to hang about for, so I think she will now leave the world of people and enter the world of ducks. The Flying Scotsman has been lovingly restored to its former glory and I will now do my best to see the same love is given to the Mallard.

It will be my birthday tomorrow. I am looking forward to being seventy-three years young. My father died at the age of seventy-one but I am just now looking forward to starting my proper life. I have still had no word from Lucy. I don't know what is stopping her from communicating with me. Maybe she just needs more time to catch up with events.

**Tuesday 8th November 2016**. I wrote again to Lucy yesterday and I decided to include the letter here for your interest.

Monday 7<sup>th</sup> November 2016

Lucy Lawless,
c/o Xena – Warrior Princess Fan Club
Creation Entertainment,
217 S. Kenwood Street,
Glendale,
CA 91205-1634, U.S.A.


My Darling Lucy,

My best bet at the moment is that you are frightened of entering a relationship based on love. Well, so am I. Your husband must have hurt you bad for you to feel about him the way you do. The best way for you to treat him is to forget him and enjoy the love of another man, in this case ME. That will hurt him more than anything else. There is no point in it for you to be considering his feelings. He doesn't deserve you.

I can't offer you a glamorous lifestyle, YET, but I can put a roof over your head, food in your belly and clothes on your back. I checked on the internet, and there are loads of two-bedroom houses for sale in Scotland within my price range, which is below £30,000. I'd like to sit down with you at the computer and pick and choose what houses we'd like, then make arrangements to go and visit them.

I shall know in January next year how well *My Journey There* is selling and how much I stand to gain in royalties. *My Journey Back – Part 1* is with the publishers at the moment and *My Journey Back – Part 2* is still on my computer. The computer I am using at the moment is a

71

Lenovo but it has had the internet feature removed, so I can only use it as a word processor at the moment. When I am free, I shall have the full internet at my fingertips, and then I will be able to upload my music onto Amazon and Apple i-tunes websites. Then, hopefully, I shall make some money as a songwriter. My voice is knackered at the moment by a dry mouth and throat, which has given me a speech impediment. This is all due to the so-called antipsychotic drugs they force me to take in here.

I want to remind you of a verse in one of MY songs:-

"The bravest thing in the whole wide world that a man or a woman can do is to love again knowing how much it hurts if the romance should fall through."

Bless you, Darling
I Love You,


<u>Bob Brooks Strong XXXXX</u>


Yesterday I did not take the Risperidone tablets that Doctor Madre prescribed because their effect on me is horrendous. I could hardly walk a straight line and I couldn't concentrate on anything, not even my music. I told Jim, my music tutor, that I am going to call it a day after the next concert, which will be in December. I was supposed to have a music session yesterday but I didn't go because I just didn't feel up to it.

When I told the staff here this morning that I was refusing to take the Risperidone, they called me in to speak to Daisy and she said that they would get Doctor Mouse to speak to me and that he would insist I take a depot. Injection. I feel as though the sword of Damocles is hovering over my head at the moment. Any time now they will call me in to speak to Mouse and then march me away to have an injection.

One thing worth mentioning here is that I am now sure that my mother, Dolly, has now departed the world of human beings and she is now on the next journey of hers in the world of ducks. So it is now time to close this chapter with a final 'Goodbye Dolly'.

**Thursday 10th November 2016**. It seems I spoke too soon, yet again. My mother has broken the spell that ties her to the world of ducks. She gave me a vision of herself as a young woman, sitting down with me at the computer and choosing houses to visit. This was exactly my vision of how things might be with me and Lucy. There are no words to describe how much I want TO GET RID OF DOLLY. (There goes that caps lock button again). I now have to wait for my people to get together yet again and try again to make a duck out of her. We must keep at it and keep trying until she is gone. I am sure we will get there soon. We are making the world of humans so unpleasant for her that she will be glad to go. That is no worse than what she did to me, so I'll say it again, "Goodbye Dolly."

To change the subject, I never did see Doctor Mouse, but another on-call psychiatrist. This guy said to me that if I didn't take the tablets of Risperidone, then I would have to suffer an injection of the same stuff. Under these circumstances I decided to take the tablets. Doctor Madre will be back on Monday and Daisy is trying to organise a meeting with Doctor Madre for me as soon as possible.

Daisy is no longer my primary nurse. She introduced me to my new primary nurse yesterday, a Chinese girl called Cindy. Last month I bought a supply of collagen tablets because I've heard that they help relieve the pain of arthritis. I still suffer from osteoarthritis in my hips, but the sciatica has gone completely thanks to the acupuncture treatment. The staff won't let me have my collagen tablets without some kind of approval. The GP won't say yes or no to me having collagen pills, so they decided to consult the dietician. I am still waiting to see the dietician.

**Sunday 20th November 2016**. It is human nature to get the alpha female together with the alpha male. In the whole wide world, that seems to be my mother, Dolly, and myself. The social pressure for me to have sex with my late mother's spirit is enormous. It has even been mooted that if I continue to refuse my mother, this will bring about the end of the human race. My reaction to this thought was at first, "Well, so be it." But then I thought, "If that is the case then one of the rich people who walk the earth can easily afford a million pounds to save civilisation." So I made that my price and there are now signs that my price will be met.

If the only way Dolly knows how to make a man happy is to open her legs for him, then she is pathetic. I have made her realise that Lucy is my soulmate, not her and the only way that she can make me happy is to leave the world of humans and enter the world of ducks. There are now signs that Dolly will do this after I have had a final dance with her. She wants me to accept that she really does love me before she goes. Lucy understands my situation and, like me, she will close her mind and think of the money. It would certainly be nice to be financially secure for the rest of our lives and to buy a nice house in a nice district where we can live.

The guy who saw me while Doctor Madre was on holiday had the name Doctor Newman. He suggested I itemise my list of the effects of the Risperidone and bring it to the next MDT meeting. For your information, I am now going to include it in this narrative.

The Effects of Risperidone
Robert Strong. November 2016.

1. Suppression of sexual functioning. I cannot even get
    an erection, let alone 'dance' with a woman.

2. Dry mouth and throat. This is the most apparent effect of the dehydration caused by the drug. This has caused me to have a speech impediment. I sometimes find it hard to speak coherently, let alone do any singing.
3. Tiredness and lethargy. This causes a lack of energy and the will to do things necessary for day to day life. Even the slightest bit of pressure is magnified to a point where I can't cope with it. This is present every waking moment.
4. A disturbed sense of balance. The effect is similar to being drunk. I can barely walk in a straight line or stand still for any length of time.
5. Overweight. In common with most antipsychotic drugs, it causes the patient to have a swollen belly and this results in being clinically obese.
6. Blurred vision. A film develops over the eyes and this makes life very difficult. It becomes hard to see what you are reading when you are holding a newspaper or book.

I am a seventy-three-year-old man and I think psychiatrists should hang their heads in shame for treating a man of my age this way.

I saw Doctor Madre and Daisy last week and gave them each a copy of the above document, so they can study it before the MDT meeting on Wednesday 23rd November.

I think they will agree to my request for a trial period off the drugs, as I can't dance with Dolly or anybody else while I am on the accursed stuff. And getting me to have mental sex with my mother is what the whole of the last seventy-three years has been all about; including the last forty years as a mental patient.

I think Dolly understands now that if my happiness is what is important to her, then she must go away and leave Lucy and me to enjoy our lives together.

I don't know if my mother has a soulmate but if she does then I hope she finds him. The same goes for my father, Frank Brooks. Bless you, Dad, all is forgiven, both ways I hope.

**Wednesday 23rd November 2016**. I was called in to the MDT meeting this morning and although Doctor Madre would not say so, and she continues to pretend that me having sex with my late mother is not what it is all about, she agreed to give me a trial period without the drugs. I am sure that if I keep Dolly sweet, I will stay off the drugs. I wrote again to Lucy this afternoon and told her that I think our best tactic is for me to appeal to my mother's better nature and simply point out to her that Lucy is my soulmate and that means letting go of me to enjoy life with Lucy.

**Thursday 24th November 2016**. Yesterday, Doctor Madre said she would give me a trial period without the antipsychotic drugs, but yesterday evening I was given the pill as before and now it seems that I will be weaned off the drug slowly, starting Monday.

I have been given a date for my operation. I will have what they call a pre-op on Monday of next week and then the operation will go ahead next Thursday. There is a sixty per cent success rate to this operation so I am asking all my friends to pray for me on Thursday morning next week. I don't believe in luck. What most people call 'luck' is actually the will of the gods manifesting itself, so promise them plenty of ambrosia and nectar if I pull through OK and make sure you live up to your promises. Maybe I should just mention that ambrosia and nectar are the food and drink of the gods.

**Friday 25th November 2016**. They have already started to wean me off the Risperidone. I did not get a tablet yesterday evening although I did get a tablet this morning. I don't think Doctor Madre knows whether she is coming or going! The old girl is still carrying on with this baloney about 'mental illness'. She refuses to concede that making a motherfucker out of me is what they have been trying to do for so many years; and the drugs have just been their way of bullying me into having sex with my mother.

I saw the dietician earlier this morning and she is letting me have my collagen tablets. Apparently Doctor Madre has to decide the dosage of collagen I get, but that is written on the box anyway, so I am looking forward to having some relief from the arthritis in my hips that I suffer from. Since I decided to dance with Dolly, my mother, lots of people are now being nice to me. I'll soon find out whether or not my mother really loves me. If she does, then she will want me to be happy, in which case she will let me go to be with Lucy and disappear herself from my world.

I have not had any Risperidone this evening, which is some small relief, but I don't think it will be enough for me to get any sexual joy yet.

I sleep in my recliner these days as it is much more comfy than my bed. This afternoon I bought a throw to drape over the recliner and keep it clean. I'm now looking forward to a good night's kip on my recliner, I don't think Dolly has gone yet so I'll keep this chapter open until I'm sure she's gone.

**Saturday 3rd December 2016**. I went into Brixton and North Hampshire Hospital on Thursday of last week for an operation on my prostate gland. I stayed there Thursday night and came back to Alcatraz Island yesterday. I have been told that I will go back to Brixton on Tuesday or Wednesday of next week for another procedure to ascertain if Thursday's operation was successful. I have a device called a catheter attached to my penis and I have to use it to urinate. I can't pee normally at all. The catheter is easy to use and has a little tap on it, which enables me to pee. This is much better than the old style of catheter where a bag was strapped to my leg and had to be emptied when full.

I am still taking two milligrams of Risperidone every morning, which not only causes me to have a speech defect but makes it impossible to have any sexual function at all. Not that the catheter would allow any sexual function anyway!.

I think that Dolly is still hanging on in the spirit world, hoping for mental sex with me. For the above reasons, this is impossible even if I wanted it to happen, which I don't, although I conceded to dance with her as a farewell fling before she disappears from the world of human beings.

Even without the catheter and the Risperidone, I don't think Dolly's will is strong enough to keep her hanging on for sex with me. I can sense that she is already cracking under the strain and before long she will inhabit a duck's egg. It all comes down to a tug-of-war to see who has the stronger will power, and when any person or other living thing tries that with me, they lose. That is my proof of who I am, and my status as the deity.

**Wednesday 7th December 2016**. I went back to Brixton and North Hampshire Hospital this morning to have the catheter removed and to see how I could get along without any catheter at all. I spent over an hour just drinking water to fill my bladder; then trying to pee naturally. It was a partial success. I found I could produce urine in substantial quantity but there was still some retention in my bladder which I had to use a free-standing catheter to remove. The nurse said I should use the catheter three or four times a day instead of five and urinate normally as much as possible. I may have to return to the hospital next year but I'll keep on going and see what happens.

I am now taking only one milligram of Risperidone a day. I take it in the morning, but its effects last all day. I think that if I keep on with my present strategy, Dolly will turn herself into a duckling before I am called upon to have sex with her. I don't think I could have sex with her anyway. She just doesn't turn me on! Quite apart from the fact I don't even like the woman. I haven't forgiven her for deserting Dad and Bill and me in 1951. I also can't forget her refusal to visit me and comfort me in 1971 when Jasmin 2 left me and I was feeling suicidal. She said she was too busy packing her bags for her holiday in Spain to spare me any of her time.

A lot of people look up to Dolly even now. They know that it is their own fault that Dolly lives a life of sin, for egging her on, and she fell for it. Now she is to learn at first hand that unrepentant sinners go to hell.

It is my idea of hell to be made to forfeit your humanity and come back to life as an animal.

Those who would achieve salvation remember my magic word 'CARA'. Confess, Apologise, Repent and Atone for your sins. A wise person will leave enough time to repent and atone for their sins before they die.

**Sunday 11<sup>th</sup> December 2016**. I am pretty sure that Dolly has finally gone. She is now on her way to being an egg It is all over the newspapers, front page headlines, somebody's mother has died.

They could hardly have been more specific. There is a lot of genuine sympathy for Dolly, which I am trying not to take as my blame for her demise. The time has now come for Lucy and me to reap all the souls we can. I feel sure that Lucy and I are the biggest players on the world stage. I have already heard people saying, "If you can't beat 'em, 'join 'em."

The time has now come to close this chapter of *My Journey Back – Part Two* and with it the closing of the most important era in the history of the world.

# Chapter 12
# The Aftermath?

**Monday 12<sup>th</sup> December 2016**. The newspapers are screaming out for me to be released. It won't be long now before I get everything I have asked for from society. Firstly, I want Lucy Lawless to be my woman, with everything socially, emotionally and sexually that that implies. Secondly, I want the justice that I should have had forty years ago. I have distilled my wants into four headings: – Freedom, Apology, Exoneration and Compensation. I won't bore you with my plans for myself any further: except to claim the intellectual property rights to my invention, which I call a 'TEG'. This stands for Thermal Electricity Generator.

I have nursed the seed of this invention for nearly forty years and I still have faith in it. It may well prove to be the magic ingredient that solves the problem of a growing shortage of energy. Maybe people will take me and my invention seriously at long last, now that Dolly is dead AND gone.

It will cost about a million pounds to secure the worldwide intellectual property rights to my underlying idea; and about another million to build a prototype. If this works, then we will have no shortage of backers to build and market TEGs. This is what I want the compensation for; apart from the obvious things like a decent and secure house which Lucy and I will call 'Home'.

**Tuesday 13<sup>th</sup> December 2016.** When people ask me what would I like to be, I reply, "Not a politician, nor a policeman, nor an entertainer, but a businessman, working in the field of renewable solar energy." I believe billions of megawatts of electricity are wasted every minute of every day by the heat of the sun falling on untapped earth. I have decided to make it my mission to tap some of this energy, and my TEGs are the equipment which, I hope, will make this dream come true.

To change the subject, it is getting near Christmas and most of the patients on this ward are going to a first-class pub called The Toby Carvery, where they do an excellent dinner at a very reasonable price. I shall be joining in the festivities and I'm looking forward to my dinner which takes place today. The staff organising the event have booked our seats in advance, which only cost us a fiver each, and we pay the balance when we have had our meal.

I was due for a dental appointment yesterday morning but it had to be cancelled as we do not have enough transport, nor staff available. This was a shame because my denture is broken and it needs fixing badly. I haven't even been allowed the time to do my food shopping for the week.

**Wednesday 14ᵗʰ December 2016**. I have now been told that my dental appointment has been rescheduled for Friday morning this week. I have volunteered to pay for a taxi as they do not have a car available.

I have now been told that I can reclaim the taxi fare as it is for a special medical appointment, which the hospital accepts responsibility for. Hopefully I can do my banking and my shopping on the same outing.

My banking is only to pay in a banker's draught from the National Savings and Investments organisation in the amount of thirty thousand pounds. I have been carrying this banker's draught with me all month and I don't want it to be mislaid or otherwise troubled. I want this money in my current account so that I have it readily to hand if I want to buy something important, such as a house, for when I get discharged. This money is my life's savings and it was held for me in the form of premium bonds which I am now cashing in.

To change the subject, I still haven't heard from Lucy but I have made one important realisation. Her behaviour had me confused for many years but I have finally figured it out. Lucy does care about my feelings which is why she has been playing this game with me. I have been confused because this is the way Lucy wants me to be. I think she has been hoping that I may be able to resolve her own confusion if I solve the riddle that her behaviour has set me. Now that I have worked all this out, I have cracked the code that has been controlling Lucy's behaviour.

Lucy's behaviour will change when she reads this. I don't know in what way, but my position remains the same – I will keep on waiting until Lucy realises that I am the right man for her. In spite of everything my rivals may have against me, Lucy has her own mind and her own set of values, even though she is not the best judge of character in the world, she realises the importance of the test of time, which she and I have both been playing for the last seventeen years.

When I die, even if I die today, I will die a happy man because I have known Lucy's love.

**Thursday 15<sup>th</sup> December 2016**. I had a chat with Daisy yesterday morning and I informed her of my realisation and the fact that I do not intend to write to Lucy again – certainly not until she stops playing this game and starts behaving like a normal human being – one who responds one way or another to someone's declaration of love.

I mentioned to Daisy that when this confusion is resolved it then leaves behind our worst enemy – doubt. This means there are no guarantees in a relationship based on love. You have to have the confidence in yourself and in your partner, and trust that they feel the same way about you. A snatch of a song of my own composition called *Timing* springs to mind.

There are many things I've learned in the years I've been interned
And I'll gladly pass this wisdom on to you.
It's that love, however strong, is destined to go wrong
If one of you forgets that it takes two.

All anyone can do is to resolve to play one's own part and trust your partner that they will continue to play theirs. I believe that Lucy and I have got as much as anyone can by way of assurances that our relationship will last.

I look forward to discussing these matters with Lucy when she comes to visit me. I think the song title *She'll be coming round the mountain when she comes*, is most appropriate.

**Friday 16<sup>th</sup> December 2016**. It is now five thirty in the morning and I have already had my first cup of coffee of the day. I am looking forward to today because my dental appointment is due for one forty-five pm and I want the situation regarding my denture to be resolved. I have only half a denture in place at the moment and I have still got the rogue tooth which broke off.

I have been advised to pay for the taxi myself and claim the money back on expenses. I don't know if I will be allowed to do my banking and/or my food shopping for the week but I am going to try and fit it all in today.

To change the subject, Lucy lost the first fight with Dolly but she didn't give up and when she fought Dolly again, she was victorious. There are still a few vestiges of Dolly's personality left behind but they don't worry me because I know that Dolly is afraid of Lucy and every time Dolly tries to interfere with us, Lucy gives her a good hiding. Sooner or later Dolly will get the message and realise she is better off as a duckling than as an enemy of Me and Lucy, which is what she has been for a long time now.

This piece of writing has two strands woven into it. One is my humdrum existence as a patient in a mental hospital. And the other is the story of my attempts to win the hand of Lucy Lawless.

Both of these strands are nearing their completion as I write. My life is in Lucy's hands and her emotional life is in mine. When my mother left everything in life except her sexual desire for her boyfriend, I heard her say, "A woman has to follow her heart." I'm hoping Lucy will take this attitude.

I did tell Lucy, several months ago, that I want her to be the great woman behind the great man that I am. I could feel her emotion when she read that letter. She wants to be the great woman behind me, and the time is nearing when she will have to prove that is who she is. I'm' not going to spell it out for her. She has to realise it for herself and until she does, all those concerned will just have to wait.

**Saturday 17ᵗʰ December 2016**. Dolly is begging me to have mercy on her soul but we have been here before. If I show her compassion, she will only use it to try again to get me to have sex with her. I am not going to make Lucy suffer that. I have concluded that even with my emotional wealth, I can't afford to have mercy on Dolly. Every time I consider this problem, I remember forty years of injections, mostly in my backside, of neuroleptic drugs Being on these drugs is the most heinous torture that humans have ever devised. Partly because your suffering is hidden from visitors who only wish you well and don't understand what you are suffering. If Doctor Madre keeps her word, I will soon be free from Risperidone, which I take orally and that will be the end of a chapter in my life on neuroleptic drugs and the start of a new chapter of my life, being treated as a normal human being.

One more consideration worthy of note is Dolly's involvement in the death of Iris. Dolly herself never broke any man-made laws, she and her followers got me to do that, but she was as guilty as hell of the crime which I committed. I was almost the only one who actually had pity on Iris. All the rest of my family hated her and were overjoyed when I killed her. Dolly's part in the death of Iris is the final straw that broke the camel's back. I want to say to Iris, "Cheer up, old girl, the one to blame for your death is now about to receive the justice she deserves."

I think it was Harold Wilson who said that sometimes rough justice is the only justice available, but it is better than no justice at all.

As Maurice Ayres would say to his erstwhile girlfriend, "Never mind, duck, you'll get another chance one day."

To change the subject, the staff here eventually found a car for me to use yesterday. The dentist is sending my denture away to be mended and it should be ready for me by Tuesday of next week. My warranty for my money went into the bank OK and my only email was from a loan shark, which I quickly classified as 'spam'. I did my week's shopping at Tesco's without any trouble and I managed to keep my vocal chords moist with Diet Pepsi. All in all, it was a very productive excursion for me.

I am hoping the single tablet of Risperidone which I have to endure daily will be removed soon. If Doctor Madre is as good as her word, then it will be. When this happens I trust and expect that my sexual energy will re-establish itself so that I won't let Lucy down as far as sexual pleasure is concerned. This has been the biggest bugbear of my recent life and I want to reward Lucy for standing by me. She may have sought sexual gratification elsewhere and I wouldn't blame her if she has. I understand that a woman has her needs but I have a strong feeling that Lucy is loyal to me, and faithful. I renew my curse on Doctor Marionette Madre for keeping me on drugs for so long, knowing that I can't satisfy any woman whilst I am taking them.

This attitude of Doctor Madre stinks of my mother's involvement. She is making sure that if she can't have me, then no other woman can and Marionette Madre is complicit with my mother's attitude.

Those who are familiar with my writing know that many, many times I have been allowed to think that we have got rid of Dolly's soul and brought her back as one creature or another, only to find that she has broken my spell and resurfaced as a DISEMBODIED SPIRIT (There goes that caps lock button again.) What gives me hope though, is that every time she is less and less her old human self and more and more like a duckling. Which is what she will be soon.

I am uniquely qualified to write this story. Not many people come to manhood only to find the whole world is a giant conspiracy to turn you into a motherfucking toy boy. That is what I have found this life to be. But mother's people are out of luck though, because that is not who I am, nor ever will be. What happens when the immoveable object collides with the irresistible force? Something has got to give and it won't be me. In spite of Doctor Madre and her drugs.

All Dolly has got to offer is her dream of having me for her boyfriend. On the other hand, I am part of a couple with Lucy. We are soulmates and an attack on one of us is an attack on us both. My mother has made enemies of us both. We both have excellent motives for getting rid of Dolly. This fight will not stop until we win and Dolly has been brought back to life as a duckling, or some other creature.

Dolly cannot hide behind a veil of anonymity for very long. Wherever she tries to hide, my people will shine a light on her and expose her for what she really is – an emotionally selfish and wicked old witch who has ruined the life of her own son because of her incestuous sexual desires and who has never even ventured an apology for ruining my life. And some people, like Doctor Madre, are still seeing the world as she wants them to see it, in spite of the truth which I have revealed.

Madre and the rest of the psychiatric community have got a lot of back-pedalling to do if they want to enjoy a peaceful afterlife when they die.

# Chapter 13
## Goodbye Dolly – 3

**Monday 19ᵗʰ December 2016**. In the previous book to this one, I discuss in some detail my conflict with Satan. I made it crystal clear that I have trounced him into a situation from which, if we are sensible, he will never recover. By confronting him and overpowering him, I got him into spirit form and then I was Field Marshall of the armies that turned him irreversibly into a dog.

In so doing, I saved the human race from the threat of extinction at his hands. I proved that EVERY MAN, WOMAN AND CHILD IN THE WORLD OWES ME THEIR LIFE. (I put the caps lock on that time myself.)

I am now calling in that debt. I want everyone who knows the truth about this situation and does not like being in debt, to help me in my conflict with my mother. Those who have read and understood the last few chapters of this book will know where I'm coming from.

I want you all to help me turn Dolly, irreversibly, into a duck. I want her protected as such from the dangers that ducks are heir to in all stages of their development. It is now 4.38 am and I want the conception of Dolly as a duck to take place at first light this morning. We must stuff her soul into a sperm cell of a randy drake and provide him with a suitable mate and then, 'Hey Presto'! Bob's your uncle!

Most people will be on their way to work at first light this morning. I will be scanning the vibes I get from duck farms to find a suitable drake and then it will be up to everybody who wants to repay their debts to me to do the rest.

I have heard the word 'Aylesbury' whispered as the location of the drake and its mate. This makes sense to me.

Those who are still on Dolly's side in this conflict are backing a loser. And that is what they will do for the rest of their lives – back losers. – until I see fit to pardon them. Those who repay their debt to me, will find that if they are careful and prudent, then they will be in a financial situation whereby they can repay their material debts – given enough time of course., but the pendulum is swinging our way now.

I have one more thing to add to this chapter at the moment and it is addressed to Dolly and her supporters. <u>This is what you get for trying to turn the Lord God Almighty into a motherfucking toy boy.</u>

When people ask me, "What was the real reason why you killed Iris?" I am now in a position to answer, "To prove who I am." And when they say, "Who are you then?" My answer is simple, "I AM THE KING."

**Tuesday 20th December 2016**. During the day, yesterday, I got the firm impression that my people from all over the world were fighting to turn Dolly into a duck. Dolly's supporters surprised me both in their strength and in their numbers, but my people definitely won the day. On the telly last evening, the media were all broadcasting Dolly's propaganda, but anyone with their ear to the ground will know that the ordinary people were not swayed by the media. The ordinary men and woman of Great Britain (and people from all over the world) are on the side of me and Lucy. They know that I and Lucy are the real King and Queen.

I haven't watched much television today, but what little I have seen tells me that the media are still on Dolly's side. The fact that they are not assisting my cause in any way tells me we have got them rattled.

I think Dolly died about ten years ago at the age of ninety. For the last four years of her life she suffered from Alzheimer's disease. This meant that she had totally lost her memory. She could not recognise even the people she was closest to in life, such as her husband, Maurice Ayres. My brother, Bill, urged me not to attempt to visit her because she would not have recognised me.

After she died, her mind and spirit became reunited and she remembered that she was fighting to get me to have sex with her. She would do this by ruining my relationships with other women so that I was facing life alone, then she would visit me to try to seduce me.

The next few sentences are my conjecture. I may be wrong, but this is what I feel is happening.

Last night I got the impression that Dolly was explaining herself to me. She explained that she had been forcing me to fight her to prove to the world my strength and my powers of leadership. This did not surprise me, for I knew that my situation and my reaction to it were Churchillian in their nature. I felt as if I were giving my people a 'We will never surrender' speech.

Now that this has been proven, Dolly has nothing left to teach me and Mother Nature has intervened again by separating Dolly's mind from her spirit. She has lost the former and the latter is on its way back to life as a duckling. A disembodies spirit, hoping to be conceived and brought back to life again must, of necessity, lose its memory of its former life so that it can start again with as clean a slate as possible.

One thing I want to mention here is that years ago there was a pop song called *China in Your Hand*. This song was very popular in the UK but I did not feel as though it pertained to me. That has now changed. Yesterday and today I have felt the weight of the colossal numbers of people in China who have answered my call to repay their debt to me. This is a big and heartfelt 'Thank you' to the people of China for answering my call. You won't regret it.

**Friday 23rd December 2016.** I haven't made an entry for the last few days because anyone who wants to know the score has only to read any of the national newspapers in the country to assess the mood of the ruling clique. Dolly and her people are looking defeat in the face and it is driving them all mad.

They are clutching at straws only to find that the straws are going down as well.

On a personal level, I had a CPA meeting on Wednesday. (That is psychospeak for a case conference.) At the meeting I asked Doctor Madre to take me off the Risperidone altogether. I am only on one milligram per day as it is. Madre agreed to this and yesterday I thought I was free of the stuff. But the charge nurse called me in to tell me my primary nurse, Cindy, has to draw up a care plan for me to sign as well as all my care team, and until this has taken place I am still on the one milligram per day dosage of the stuff. It is going to take a few days due to the Christmas break to get the contract drawn up and signed, so I have another week or so before I am off the poison.

Yesterday morning, I thought I wasn't going to have to take it anymore, and I conveyed this thought to Lucy. Lucy was delighted because it seemed as though I would be getting my sex drive back, but when I heard about the contract, it became apparent that Lucy and I would have another week or so to wait before we can get it together sexually. I hated having to disappoint Lucy in this way but that was just another parting shot from Dolly and her people.

I still have a bit of a speech defect and my denture is broken and is being mended by the dentist's people. I won't be able to collect the mended denture until the new year. Hopefully, I will be off all antipsychotic medication by then and I won't be suffering dehydration of the mouth and throat, which is one of the effects of the drug. I am sure that most of my complaints will disappear when I have been off the drug for a while.

I have withdrawn from the music sessions that I have been attending on Monday afternoons. I had a damning report from the occupational therapist who attends these sessions, but I had withdrawn from the sessions already before I heard his report. I have got my criticisms of him as well but I am not going to get into an argument with him or the OT department. I stayed with the band until the concert which we performed at the

Christmas 'Fun Week', but that is all the free music they are going to get from me.

I have resumed my guitar practice on my own as a solo artiste. I want to push my own songs as well as my choice of songs to do cover versions of. When I have got my speech back to normal, I may resume doing concerts both in Alcatraz Island and in The old folks Nursing Home. I am pretty sure though, that by the time I have overcome my speech defect, I will have an absolute discharge from mental hospitals and I will be together with Lucy.

I am confident that my mother's soul will inhabit the body of a duck before long, and I will get the recognition that I have fought for for so long. When Dolly disappears, I will be the King and it will be up to me and Lucy to decide what to do about it.

**Saturday 24<sup>th</sup> December 2016**. I have a couple of impressions of myself on file and I am now recalling them. They are of my likes and dislikes in the culinary field and are easy to access. When I am King a lot of people will be interested in them and also in my books. Olympia Publishers are taking a long time over *My Journey Back – Part One*. This is probably because I asked them to get copyright holder's permission to use some snatches of songs which have influenced me in life. It is not always easy to identify who is the copyright holder of a piece of music.

It is over three months since I wrote to Olympia Publishers abought the copyrights holder's permission to use snatches of a song in my book, *My Journey Back – Part One*. I have therefore written to them again but it seems as though everything has stopped for Christmas. I won't post the letter until Tuesday as by then, the post should be back to normal.

Yesterday's entry in this book has spurred the media into generating a mood of calm and goodwill. Dolly's people have recruited all the international leaders they can persuade to join their cause, BUT IT WON'T DO THEM ANY GOOD. THEY ARE ALL GOING DOWN IN THE NEAR FUTURE. (That caps lock button has a mind of its own!) Dolly has taken advantage of the fact that I am her son to steal my throne in the spirit world. Now I am claiming it back and there is nothing she nor anyone else can do to stop me. My supporters constitute the vast majority of the adult members of the human race.

We do not yet control the media but the thoughts and feeling of the vast majority of men and women are on my side. We don't trust the media, nor believe them.

I don't know much about the breeding programmes of duck farmers. It may be that we will have to wait until the spring of 2017 before the sap starts rising in the drakes, and we can get Dolly reborn as a duckling. This is a small inconvenience compared to the reward that will soon be ours.

A friend of mine in a mental hospital in Yorkshire wrote to me a Christmas card and it transpires he is on a ward called 'Mallard Ward'. I have mentioned before that a mallard is a wild duck. If, as it seems, Dolly is to become a mallard, then we won't need to worry about the duck farmers. We must, instead, keep a weather eye open for the migratory patterns of wild ducks.

**Sunday 25th December 2016**. Happy Christmas everyone. (Except Dolly and her followers.) Spiritually, they are no longer people. They are the enemies of God's people. They have picked a fight with God! The fools. Soon they will have lost this fight and then the universe will know who the boss is.

**Monday 26th December 2016**. I awoke at about midnight, and it is now 1.35 am. I discovered a duckling hiding behind the back of this building. I am pretty sure this is what Dolly is now. I told my people yesterday that I wouldn't consider their debt repaid until Dolly became a duckling. I think they took me at my word and did the business for me. Well done folks. You won't regret it. Consider your debt to me repaid! From now on, all our fortunes will improve and those of Dolly's supporters will get worse.

I did the right thing in asking my supporters for help. They gave it to me. I can now reclaim my throne in heaven and consider the insurgency, led by my mother, as over now. I put the duckling I found along with the other ducklings. From now on, she has got to learn the way of ducks for her own survival. I'm sure she will make it as a duck.

Dolly has proved me wrong so many times when I thought we had beaten her but this time it is not just me, it is the whole human race that has transmorphed her. I think I can close this chapter now and concentrate on winning the hand of the woman I love – the wonderful actress, Lucy Lawless.

I have now read some of today's newspapers and I got the unmistakeable impression that my thoughts of early this morning are, in fact, correct. Their mood is sombre as the ruling clique is mourning its leader, Dolly. One good sign from my point of view is that Lord King got a mention. He is an ex-leader of the Bank of England. This is my announcement that I am on the scene now and I am not wasting any time. I will not tolerate any of my rivals exploiting Dolly's demise.

# Chapter 14
## More thoughts on the future

**Monday 26th December 2016.** 'A Happy Wife makes for a Happy Life'. This is a quotation that should ring bells for a lot of married men. It is one I feel all men should be made aware of whenever they get married. It will, I hope, bring a lot of happiness into the world and inspire a lot of married people with some food for thought.

Lucy is the great woman behind the great man I am.

I think that one of my tasks is to prove who I am to the people of America. Many of them already know, so it is up to me to inspire them to have some missionary zeal and to get them to persuade their countrymen (and woman) to read and understand my books.

I would like to see the legend, 'In God We Trust' reinstated on high value currency notes. Those who know the truth, know that I deserve this, by my actions in this life as well as all my former lives. I am still the same person.

To change the subject, Cindy has not been in work today so I haven't had the chance to ask her how she is getting on with writing my care plan. The charge nurse realised why I wanted to talk to her so he informed me that she should be in, with the finished care plan, on Thursday. He has, apparently, criticised her original care plan and suggested some changes. The care team members should all be in on Thursday as well so hopefully we can get all the paperwork boxed off on Thursday and I can start my drug free trial on Friday of this week, the 30th December. I'm sure I will get my sex drive back when I come off the medication so this will be good news for

Lucy as well as me. All the sacrifices we have had to make will, I am sure, prove to be worthwhile.

**Tuesday 27<sup>th</sup> December 2016**. I am looking forward to the reaction of the followers of Islam when they discover that God (or Allah as they call me) is an Englishman! Will they still say, 'Allah Akbar' (God is Great)? One worthwhile thought of mine is that I no longer have to prove my greatness, just my identity. I can do that to the satisfaction of most reasonable people by pointing to the fact that I got the better of Satan when no other man could confront him and win! The Devil is no longer a threat to the survival of our species, thanks to me.

That is what the song *Lily the Pink* is all about.

**Wednesday 28<sup>th</sup> December 2016**. Cindy was in work yesterday and she had brought with her the care plan for my drug free trial. I signed both copies and tomorrow Doctor Madre will sign them. I spoke to the MDT this morning and it was agreed that my Risperidone tablet tomorrow morning will be my last one. After that I will be drug free, although I will have to be extra careful in what I do and say or I might be put back on the stuff. Psychiatry exists to cover up the spiritual facts of life. I know the truth but I can't say it or they will make me take these obnoxious drugs again.

Those who have read my books will understand. After forty years of torment at the hands of the psychiatric profession, I have had enough.

Now that Dolly is dead AND gone, the old guard are still controlling the media. Some people are still being condescending and patronising towards me but I am making plans to get rid of them. There was an American man named Sam who ran America for several decades before he died. They even named their country after him. They called it 'Uncle Sam'. The British old guard became leaderless when we got rid of Dolly so they have turned to Uncle Sam to lead them. This is reflected in the name of the new manager of Crystal Palace Football Club. The new manager's name is Sam Allerdyce.

I had a word with the old soul, 'Uncle Sam', and asked him what he would like to be. I made it clear to him that anyone who leads the old guard will forfeit their humanity and be brought back as an animal. Someone put the idea into my head that Uncle Sam might like to be a kangaroo. This idea suits me fine. Uncle Sam has got today to think and act. Either he tells the old guard that he is a God-fearing man and they can all go to hell, or I will suggest to my people that our next job is to turn Uncle Sam into a kangaroo.

Tomorrow will be a big day for me and my people; either we fall out with Uncle Sam or we welcome him into our fold as another successful soul we will have saved. These soul saving sessions seem to be the way forward for my people and me. 'Saved' gets the loud hurrah!

**Thursday 29th December 2016**. I think Uncle Sam is on my side now. And I also think the old guard are running scared of me, and with good reason. One major sign that things are beginning to go my way now is a piece on telly this morning called *Good Riddance*, which is the way I and all my people feel about my late mother. The excuse for the title of the show is that this is how New Yorkers feel about the old year (2016) which is nearly over now and we are looking forward with hope for a better year to come.

I still haven't heard from Lucy. I think that will change soon though. I had my last tablet of the obnoxious drug this morning. Doctor Madre is due to sign Cindy's care plan today and that will be the start of my drug free trial. According to the choreography, I am now no longer on antipsychotic drugs. This, of course, means that I will soon get my sex drive back and then Lucy and I can start to enjoy our adult lives. It also means that the tiredness and lethargy that I have suffered for the last forty years is now over, together with a whole host of complaints about inconveniences to my body that I have suffered.

Writing this book is my way of shouting from the rooftops, "I am a free man now and there is nothing wrong with me, nor has there ever been." The last forty years have been my mother's punishment of me for refusing to have sex with her.

Now that Dolly is dead and gone, things are moving ahead for me at top speed. I'm sure that I will soon have everything I want, chiefly including Lucy.

Doctor Marionette Madre called me to the interview room earlier on today and we had a chat about the care plan for the drug-free trial. She said that she had one or two tweaks to make to Cindy's effort but these could be done immediately and that, as of NOW, I have started my drug-free trial. She made no mention of my late mother, nor her fate, but it is obvious to me that that is the real reason for the drug-free trial at this time.

I am not yet in a position to thump the table and say, "Give me justice, NOW!" but I am angling to get myself into that position. Until then, I will still have to wait for the four things I want by way of justice. I am hoping that when *My Journey Back – Part One and Part Two*, become published and well-read then there will be enough understanding of my story to persuade the jury of my cause.

The purpose of psychiatry is to cover up the spiritual truths of life, but in order to get off the drugs and to get my freedom, I will have to pretend that I don't know this.

I will be going to bed soon but this time tomorrow I'll be hoping for a dance with Lucy before I go to sleep. I should have enough of my sex drive back to achieve this and it will be without unwanted intrusion from my late mother. If other people want a share of the happiness that Lucy and I enjoy, then Men, imagine you are me; and Women, imagine you are Lucy and we'll all come together.

**Friday 30th December 2016**. I did not have any antipsychotic medication this morning, so my drug-free trial is underway. Today's *Daily Mail* carried the headline 'It's Not Over Yet'. So I suspect that the old guard have one or two tricks up their sleeve which they have yet to play on me. But that doesn't worry me greatly. I am more than a match for them!

I wrote to my solicitor earlier on this morning, asking her to apply for a Mental Health Tribunal hearing as soon as possible and to apply for an absolute discharge for me. I expect the tribunal panel will want to do things by the book, so they will grant me my discharge.

Now that I am off the drugs, and my mother is now dead and gone, I'm hoping that Lucy will contact me soon. If she doesn't then I'll just get on with my own plans for my life. When I get discharged, I plan to buy a small house in Scotland, where the property is cheap and to continue with my writing, my music and my quest for justice. If Lucy still doesn't want to know me, then I may take another partner, just to keep me company, but Lucy will always be my soulmate.

**Saturday 31st December 2016**. There is a saying that hell hath no fury like a woman scorned. I rejected my mother's sexual advances to me and the price she made me pay for that was to be driven to homicide, then to spend forty years in captivity and be tormented with neuroleptic drugs which stifle all your sexual feelings, amongst many other horrible effects. She is a duckling now and I have no regrets about making her forfeit her humanity in her next life. That is the worst hell I can imagine. Maybe one day, I'll give her another chance as a human being, but it won't be for another forty years at the earliest.

It is New Year's Eve tonight but I expect I'll be too tired to see the New Year in. I'm told that the drugs which I have been taking take weeks to get out of your system, so I'm not expecting any great changes in the immediate future, just a lengthy wait until I get all my faculties back.

One good thing which I thought worth a mention is that the operation on my prostate gland, which took place earlier this month, is now looking like it was successful. I am getting near to the stage where I can pass my urine naturally all the time. I have only to use the catheter once or twice a day at the moment, which is a big improvement on last month when I couldn't urinate naturally at all. I had a letter from the hospital consultant earlier this week, giving me a date for my next appointment with him in June 2017, so the people at the hospital must realise that it needs time for the operation to have its full effect.

The acupuncture treatment which I had earlier this year completely cured my sciatica and the collagen tablets which I now take twice a day have almost completely got rid of the pain caused by the osteoarthritis. Now that I am off the so-called antipsychotic drugs, I'm getting back to good health.

**Sunday 1st January 2017.** Happy New Year to almost everybody. I have a strong feeling that this is going to be a good year for me. Now that my mother is dead and gone, people will take me as they find me, instead of being told how to treat me by a jealous old woman.

**Wednesday 4th January 2017.** I've been off the drugs for nearly a week now and there doesn't seem to be much change. I still find it hard to get any kind of sexual activity, I can't even get an erection. I think this is one of the effects that will take a long time to put right.

I went all day yesterday without having to resort to the catheter once. I tried again today but last night I kept on waking up because I wanted to pee. In the small hours of the morning, I used the catheter and got a reading of 1400 mil. This precluded attempts to pee naturally and I managed to get a few hours' sleep.

I have stopped writing letters to Lucy because she never replies and I think I know why. I think she sees me as a member of a generation which has oppressed her and the only way she can score points off us is to be insolent. Her behaviour is that of an insolent girl, not that of a courageous woman, which is what I want her to be, and what I think she will be when she grows up. The only way I can think of to help her is to stop writing to her. I have had enough of her insolence. I think she must write to me now and if she doesn't then there is no hope of a relationship between Lucy and me. I say this even though I still think of her as my soulmate. Perhaps the age gap between us is too great for an emotional relationship between us. She was the one who waited twenty-four and a half years after my birth before she came into the world. So she has only got herself to blame if nothing comes of a union between us.

It was Aphrodite who made me think that Lucy and I were destined to settle down together but at the moment it seems like Lucy is proving Aphrodite wrong. Something has got to happen and it has got to come from Lucy. All I can do is wait and hope but if I get my discharge soon, as seems likely, then I will buy a small house in Scotland and I expect I will take some other woman for a partner if Lucy still doesn't want to know me.

I am still waiting to hear from Olympia Publishers concerning the publication of *My Journey Back – Part One*. I have waited for three months since I asked them to try and get copyright permission to quote from *Lily the Pink*. I have therefore decided to re-write the passages in the book where I have used copyrighted material. It's a shame because *Lily the Pink* and other songs have had a big influence on me, but I can't afford to wait any longer. I want to get this book, *My Journey Back – Part Two* off to the publishers, but I want them to get Part One ready for publication first. I haven't even started doing the proofreading yet, nor had the cover illustration done.

# Chapter 15
## God's in Charge

**Saturday 21st January 2017**. It has been three weeks since I made an entry in this diary. A lot has happened but I will deal with the most significant thing first. You will recall from chapter 13 that I recalled the debt that the human race owes me. Unfortunately, it was not paid satisfactorily. About ten days ago, I was dancing with Lucy when, shortly before I was about to climax, I felt my mother's spirit, yet again trying to seduce me. I stopped short of letting my mother succeed and gave my orgasm to Lucy. I nonetheless felt the influence of what my mother was doing to me and I made the important decision that MY WILL MUST REMAIN PARAMOUNT.

I considered trying again to turn Dolly into a duckling but I reasoned that it is going to take another couple of months before the drakes are again fertile. I thought of writing again to Lucy and asking her to be patient for another couple of months, but then I reasoned, as I had on a previous occasion, that rats copulate at all times of the year and at all times of the day and night. I therefore broadcast again to my people and told them to help me turn Dolly irreversibly into the offspring of a rat. What then surprised me was that it took only a couple of minutes from finding a randy rat to the completion of the endeavour.

Dolly's last words before she finally disappeared from humanity were, "God's in charge."

**Monday 23rd January 2017**. My mother was a sinful and decadent woman. She was influenced by Satan and embraced and condoned pleasure seeking at whatever cost to anyone else's happiness. Her favourite idea of pleasure seeking was to have incestuous relationships with her sons, mainly myself.

Not until the very end did she believe in God or that God has a higher purpose for mankind than hedonistic pleasure seeking. The last thing she realised was that her own son, me, is indeed God.

My mother paid the price for embracing and condoning decadence. I made her forfeit her very humanity. I can think of nothing worse that can happen to a person than that. That is my idea of hell and that is the fate that awaits all unrepentant sinners. They come back as animals in their next lives.

My mother was a hugely influential woman upon society in Great Britain and the wider world. She was the real matriarch of society even though her power was all indirect and applied from 'behind the scenes'. Her own overt fame was very limited to being a councillor on Lambeth Borough Council in south London. She was hugely popular and used her influence to help people and win friends. She used to get hundreds of cards at Christmas time.

What I found out for myself was that she got all her friends, both those she knew personally and her huge army of people who would have been lost souls, but for their belief in *her*, to influence *me* into complying with her will. This resulted in all my relationships turning out to be unhappy ones and the day was to come when I realised the immense iniquitous truth that her huge popularity and influence was all founded upon making my life a misery. That was how all those people got their sexual pleasure. They got it from their guilt at what they were doing to *me*. No wonder I had such an unhappy life.

Future generations of human beings can be thankful that I was able to find the superhuman courage to shoulder the burden of society's guilt. We are all sinners, including me, and we all like to believe that if we are truly sorry then we can be forgiven. I killed my stepmother, Iris. Although there were many influences that were to blame, principally my mother, it was *me* who performed the terrible deed and I am truly sorry to Iris for depriving her of all the years of life she may have had were it not for me.

It was my mother's decadent moral leadership of society that enabled homosexuals and lesbians to get their sordid activities legitimised. Everybody knows that this is against the will of God, but few people are sufficiently God-fearing enough to take notice of that. YET. It wasn't just Dolly's influence. There are a lot of corrupt people in high places in society and they too had a lot to do with the filth that so many people are wallowing in at the moment. People who would be good people were it not for the weak leadership from successive church leaders and the ostensible leaders of society, namely the Queen and her main successors.

I expect to live for another thirty years and in that time I have two main jobs to perform. One of them is to clean up society and give Great Britain and any other country that accepts my leadership, a decent and happy population. People who have a purpose in life and enjoy the fruits of their labour by living lives of prosperity and peace. People who raise their children properly to cherish human values and who live with love in their lives. I am sure that people will read my words and think about them for themselves. I do not want people to be mental slaves who obey God's will because that is what I say. I want people to be led by those who think about the meaning of life. Those who realise what makes us better than animals. Those who understand what it is to really love other people and care for them.

The other job that my life is all about at the moment (and will be for quite a while), is to make a woman out of Lucy Lawless. Lucy is a wonderful girl but she is nearly forty-nine years old at the moment. That is the age I was when I first proved myself. I think it will take Lucy a bit longer because she has many childish attitudes still, and she doesn't seem to have had much management of her life so far.

It was Lucy herself who gave me this job, without even knowing it consciously herself. It was Lucy who waited twenty-four and a half years after I was born before she came into the world. She waited so long because she knew that she would need the love and guidance of an older man to help her fulfil her destiny and discover who she is. A man who has experience of life and is a deep thinker. A man who has acquired much wisdom and knows that his purpose is to teach Lucy everything he can about the meaning of life and what it really means to be human.

And by 'teaching', I don't just mean intellectually. Life isn't just something you learn about by reading, nor by discussion, you learn about it by living it; by really strong emotions and by really caring about other people.

I fully expect that in teaching Lucy, I will learn a lot myself.

**Wednesday 25th January 2017.** At this point in this narrative, I want to make a few observations about society in Great Britain at the moment. Dolly's huge army of followers haven't yet disappeared. They are still writing the newspapers and they are still broadcasting on the radio. In the papers they are still using techniques of subliminal suggestion to promote my decadent mother's filthy attitudes.

When I was a boy there was a popular song called *Living Doll* and another one called *Hello Dolly*.

These songs were just one small part of the colossal promotional effort that went into making my mother the real sex symbol of the era she lived in. It was my misfortune that I was the boy she was determined to have sex with, whether I liked it or not.

Yesterday they played *Living Doll* on the radio and in the programme there was a character named Bobby, which was what they used to call me when I was a boy. This kind of pathetic nonsense is their attempt to, even now, rub my nose in my late mother's filth. But these people are living in the past. They are batting on a losing wicket. They still worship a goddess who no longer exists and consequently all their hopes and dreams are now turning into fears and nightmares. All these people have been so horrible to me for so long that I must say that I now find their plight a source of amusement they are now getting what they deserve and I don't just say, "Good job too." I want them to know that I find their situation hilarious.

I too have a huge army of sympathisers who share my thoughts and feelings about what has been going on and what now needs to be done to make this country, and this world, a fit place for human beings to live in.

What my mother never realised in all her life and the dwindling band of idiots who still worship her still don't realise, is that immorality always brings about far more misery than the pleasure it tries to seduce people with. Allowing oneself to be seduced in this way is a weakness that most people, including me, have at some time in their life succumbed to, but anyone worth their salt sees through this deceptive trick and resolves to be more sensible in future. Most people find they can be if they try.

Immorality then is something that we cannot deny exists, so people of good sense have found a purpose for it. Its purpose is to help us test our children and make them see the error of the ways of people who are stupid and/or just weak. It is the job of religious leaders to help these people and to teach them the error of their ways.

I have been harping on a bit about immorality because I have had my face rubbed in it for so long by my mother and other members of my family, principally the older generation, that my reaction to it has become a significant part of my thoughts.

However, I now want to tell you some things about myself. In spite of the emotional cruelty that I had inflicted on me as a child, and as an adolescent, I still love the human race. In spite of all their weaknesses and failings, they are MY people and I love them. At the dawn of humanity, I was Adam; the father and progenitor of the human race. They are MY creation and they are the envy of all other living things.

Satan and other false gods, such as my mother, would destroy humanity through decadence, sin and perversion. If these evil ones had their way mankind would become weak and stupid, no longer dominant and at serious risk of extinction. I will not allow that to happen to my people. We are here to protect the future of mankind, for that is also OUR future. We must make our children see life the same way so that they in turn will protect the generation to come after them and so on, until this earth eventually is destroyed by cosmic forces when our sun becomes a super nova. That will not happen for billions of years yet, so we have time to figure out what to do about it when it eventually starts to happen.

We must give our children love and when they start to grow up, we must teach them the difference between love and sex. That was something my mother never discovered. We must protect and perpetuate the taboos of humanity such as the laws against incest, for these taboos have protected humanity since the dawn of the human race and will continue to do so as long as the leaders of people are wise enough to realise their purpose. My mother was the leader of her generation but she wasn't wise enough to follow my teachings as they are written in the Bible. My teachings have not changed greatly since then. My mother thought she knew best, but she didn't. She thought that *her* will was the most important thing in creation; but look where that got her. It got her ratified. I want future leaders of humanity to learn from this. Know that I am God and follow MY teachings in the Bible, and in these books of mine.

This may seem to contradict what I wrote earlier about mental slavery but a wise leader will realise there is no contradiction. The right way is the right way, whether you realise it for yourself or whether you take my word for it.

I thought some of you might like to know what I am like as a person; my likes and dislikes and so on; my tastes, attitudes and opinions. In spite of my thoughts on immorality, I am a broadminded person. I haven't had physical sex for over forty years but that hasn't been my fault. I have been locked up for all that time in mental hospitals. But I am not past it and I won't be for many years yet. I am looking forward to a full married life when I get out. Which, hopefully, will be soon.

I won't deny that Lucy Lawless is the girl I love and want to marry, if she will have me. But after she digests the letter which I sent her yesterday, I think she is now going through the metamorphosis that we call 'the change of life'. I am making a woman out of her. I am confident that she will come through this change with flying colours but it will require a little time before she then sorts out her attitudes and opinions. I obviously want to know how she will feel about ME once she has become a woman. I hope with all my heart that I have made her love me. If I haven't, and she doesn't, I don't know what will become of me. I think I am too old to start again with anyone else and anyway, I have no desire to do so. Lucy will always be the one for me. There is no question of going back to the drawing board. But enough of sad thoughts. I am very optimistic that Lucy will accept that I am the man for her. She is the one that Aphrodite herself made me aware of and that Lucy and I would eventually settle down together and have a happy marriage. That is the destiny I believe will happen. When Aphrodite recommended Lucy to me, I could tell that she was jealous of Lucy, because she, herself, loves me. But she was nonetheless selfless enough to accept that Lucy and I are real soulmates.

I enjoy dancing, both with body movements and in the meaning of mental sex. I am not a great fan of ice cream, which to the uninitiated is a byword for adultery. Not even mentally. I love Lucy too much for that and always will.

I like good songs, both with good lyrics and well played musical instruments. I like some classical music but I am not a great fan of a lot of it. I find much of it is like listening to a musical score to a film but without the movie! I am not a great fan of art. I can't draw or paint to save my life. I admire the work of those who can and do it well, but most of what I've seen is pretentious rubbish. I like good food, from all nationalities. In most British towns and cities these days there is a wealth of restaurants from all over the world and with some absolutely delicious cuisine.

I also like eating in the adult meaning of the word but I believe a sensible man or woman will do so with care, for those who play with fire do sometimes get burned. My stepmother, Iris, was a case in point. She was a woman who used to feed sexually upon my spirit, and look what happened to her.

**Thursday 26<sup>th</sup> January 2017**. I like good poetry and I have written quite a bit of poetry myself, some of it quite good. I think my love poems to Lucy are good but she has yet to tell me what she thinks of them. I am a singer/songwriter/guitarist and I have been told that some of my songs are works of genius. I'm good on the guitar but my singing voice is not my strongest point. In fact, I now have a problem: for over seventy-two years I have always spoken perfectly normally. I have a London accent and I have never had a problem with speaking. But about six months ago I developed a speech defect. I don't know what caused it but I now speak with a lisp. I say 'sh' instead of 's'. I thought it might be caused by the antipsychotic drugs which these people used to make me take. It also occurred to me that it may be because I had some tooth extractions last year and I thought that might have altered the shape of my mouth. But I don't really know what caused it nor what I can do about it. The denture which I now wear doesn't help. The problem now is that if I can't even speak properly, I certainly can't sing! I've had to stop doing my concerts because of this which has upset me and my fans. I have quite a few of those! What I'm hoping now is that at some stage soon I can interest a good singer to record and promote my songs and I will have some success as a songwriter. I have written to date a total of thirty-nine songs and I have recorded them on three CDs.

I have A GOOD SENSE OF HUMOUR AND I ENJOY A GOOD LAUGH. (There goes that caps lock button again). Most of us find other people's misfortunes amusing, but I like it when they are getting their just deserts! Some humour is sick and some humour is spiteful, like that of the bastards who used to laugh at me. I find that kind of thing has nothing to recommend it. It doesn't bring any real joy to anyone.

I used to be a profession computer programmer. I enjoyed my work and I was good at it. I have a good logical brain and I am careful and meticulous in my work, which is necessary in computers. I am still a Fellow of the Institution of Analysts and Programmers, although I am retired now and I don't take an active role in the work of the institution.

I studied maths at university and although I dropped out in the third year of my course, mainly for financial reasons, I passed my exams at the end of the second year and I would have got a pass in my degree. But I am still quite proud of my academic achievement in getting that far. It is hard to study when you have a wife and kids and hardly any money and you have bills to pay.

I want to say a bit more about the attitudes and opinions of many of the people in British society at the moment. I have already stated, and I think worth stating again, that these people still worship a goddess who no longer exists. Namely my mother, Dolly. I want them to think about the consequences of this. I want them to realise that unless they change their approach to life, and their attitude to myself, then they are going to suffer terribly. They are people. And people have hopes and dreams, aspirations and ambitions. Without a real God, all these things turn to dust. They must now accept that Dolly is no longer real and they must realise for themselves that their continued belief in her is folly.

I repeat, if you worship a god that does not exist, all your hopes and dreams turn into fears and nightmares. The torment for Dolly's followers is just beginning and I have little sympathy for those who fail to see the error of their ways. THEIR REASON FOR LIVING HAS DISAPPEARED! They will contemplate suicide and some of them will do it, but some will realise that even that is no way out of their torment, for Dolly does not even exist in the spirit world.

They will eventually come to realise that I am God and that the only way out of their torment is to become God-fearing people.

Sensible people will realise that I am right, and they will not waste any time in making the changes that they must make to their approach to life. What they will have to do is find the grace to apologise to me for treating me the way they used to and resolve to treat me and my people with the love and respect that we deserve in future. Then we can begin to make this country a fit place for decent people to live in, instead of the cesspit which it is at the moment thanks to my decadent mother

**Friday 27<sup>th</sup> January 2017**. I made Satan disappear. He is now a dog. In doing so I saved the whole human race from certain doom at his hands. I think I deserve recognition and reward for this achievement and I intend to get what I want.

I made Dolly disappear. She is now a rat. She was the sex goddess of the whole adult world. Not just Great Britain, nor the English speaking world, but the whole world, including such countries as China. She was the sexual and spiritual leader of the whole human race and her importance cannot be overestimated. In making her disappear I brought about the REAL end of the era in which Dolly lived.

I have said before in this book and I think it worth saying again, that she thought her will was the strongest thing in creation. I proved her wrong. I proved that MY will is the supreme force in the Universe. Future world leaders must take notice of this. Don't think you are the REAL God, just because you are the leader of your generation of mankind. Know that I am the REAL man and the REAL boss, and know your place.

In making Dolly disappear, I took away the reason for living of a huge section of humanity. These people are going to find themselves living in misery and torment which is now only just beginning. It is going to get worse and worse for them until many of them are living in the deepest depths of dark despair and abject despondency. Everything they ever believed in will turn out to be false. Everything they ever wanted will turn out to be unobtainable and everything they ever thought they were will turn out to be a sick delusion.

Those people among them who are worth their salt will realise that their only way out of this torment is to accept that *I* am the REAL God and King, and they must now become MY people.

It may occur to some people reading this that I am now making the wording of the Lord's Prayer become true. MY kingdom is coming and My WILL shall be done on Earth as it is in Heaven. For MINE is the kingdom, the power and the glory for ever and ever, Amen.

All people must now accept, as Dolly did, too late for her, that God's in charge.

Lucy Lawless is, now I think, going through a metamorphosis. A change of life. She is no longer a girl and she is becoming a woman. A REAL woman. It will be up to her to prove what kind of woman she will be, but I believe she will prove to be a wonderful woman, Kind hearted, concerned and considerate; loving, intelligent, beautiful and someone who knows how to treat other people with the love and respect they deserve. I am sure she will turn out to be the great woman behind the great man that I am. She will be my emotional bedrock and the love of my life. I am convinced that her REAL spiritual identity is Mother Nature herself. I want the world to treat her with love and respect for I want her to be MY wife. She is my Queen and my goddess. AND YOURS.

# Chapter 16
## In conclusion

At this point in the book I am going to write a few words about some of the people I have known in my life and I am going to say what I think of them and why. Some of the things I have to say are complimentary and some are not, but nonetheless, that is the opinion that these people gave me of themselves.

My father, Frank Arthur Brooks, was a wonderful man. When I was seven years old and my mother left home, I saw him cry. He loved her and she broke his heart. I felt enormous sympathy for him even at that age. I knew she had done him wrong. He eventually found the courage to try again at marriage with Iris, for I think, that just like myself, many years later, he felt the duty to survive for the sake of his children, and he married again because of the need for us to have a mother figure. British society, led by my vindictive mother, treated him abominably all his life but he never stopped loving human beings. Even near the end of his life, his eyes were full of love, intelligence, humour, fun and laughter. He sacrificed the life of his second wife, Iris, whom he loved dearly (even though not many other people did), because he knew that this would give the human race its best chance of survival against the power of Satan. He, along with others, gave me the job of killing Iris, even though he knew that this job did not sit squarely with my nature nor my conscience. He gave the job to me because he knew that I would be the best person to fight Satan. The way things worked out, he was proved right. Satan is no more and we have survived. I hope you are proud of me, Dad and I hope the human race now treats you with the love and respect you deserve. Bless you.

Nicholas Robert Stephen Brooks was my first-born son. He was murdered by his own mother shortly before reaching the age of seven months. Even though he died at that tender age, I could tell he was an intelligent and wonderful person. His beautiful nature gave me one of the happiest experiences that I have had in my life. His mother neglected him and did not care for him. She did not hold him in her arms to feed him but laid him on his side in his cot with his bottle perched upon a pillow, leaning downwards into his mouth and she left him to feed himself at the age of not many days or weeks. When he started needing more solid food, she did not try to spoon feed him with his cereal, but she mixed it with his milk in his bottle and she then enlarged the teat with a pin and again, left him to feed himself. This behaviour of hers appalled me so, whenever I had the time, I would hold him, give him my love and affection, feed him properly and try to make him enjoy his young life as much as I could. I did not have a lot of time though, for at this time in my life I was not only working for a living but also learning my trade, which was data processing, and studying for my A levels at evening school two nights a week and also having lots of studying to do as homework. Nicky, however, appreciated my efforts to make him happy and he consequently loved me. He responded to his mother's lack of care by not loving her very much. When I used to play with him, I tried to teach him his name and my name, 'Dadda'. One day when he was five months old, I came home and when I opened the door and *he saw me, he recognised me and knew my name.* He was standing in his cot and saying, 'Dadda, Dadda, Dadda'. He was holding on to the bars of the side of the cot and jumping up and down for joy. He was laughing as he said my name and there was a huge smile on his face. He was making no secret of the fact that he was delighted to see me and his obvious love for me filled me with happiness that will stay with me forever. He and I gave each other sincere, unselfish, undoubting love.

Bill Edward Brooks is my elder brother. There was a great deal of sibling rivalry between us when we were boys. We used to fight like cat and dog. I think this was because neither of us wanted to be the lowest one in the pecking order of the family. Bill, nonetheless, was very protective towards me, his kid brother, and I loved him because he wanted to play a significant part in looking after me. I have recounted incidents of this in my first book, *My Journey There*. As we grew up, we both pursued different walks of life. We both had successes and failures. We both experienced financial hardships. We both had children and we both discovered what it really means to struggle for a goal with all your heart and soul and ability. We had the same mother, Dolly, and in the fullness of time, we both proved that we are real men. In doing so, we have earned each other's respect and admiration.

I can only guess at what was behind the titles of the two films, *Kill Bill* and *Kill Bill 2*. Dolly never could accept that her sons didn't want sex with her. She must have felt that it was because she wasn't sexy enough. The stupid woman never did understand real men.

Bill married a girl named Christine when he was in his twenties. That was about fifty years ago and Bill and Christine, who is now a wonderful woman, have stayed together ever since. I am proud of both of them for making their marriage work when so many couples are mismatched and break up. I want Bill to know I love him and that I am happy and proud to have him for my brother.

Jasmin Joy Langley, nee Brooks, nee Hill, was my first wife. She was the girl I refer to as Jasmin 1. We married when we were eighteen and it was a mismatch from the start. The marriage was engineered by my stupid mother. Dolly 'gave' me to her because she was sycophantic towards Dolly. This pleased Dolly's vanity and Dolly continued to try and bind me to her all her life. She was not the kind of girl I wanted for a wife. She wasn't very intelligent and she was lacking in human qualities, particularly maternal instincts. That is why I left her.

She not only murdered Nicky, but she was also a bad mother to our other two sons, Anthony and Christopher. She was a sweet kid in some ways and she did acknowledge my leadership qualities and looked to me for leadership. On one occasion she gave me a birthday card with the words 'To the Captain of our Ship' written on it. It contained a picture of a ship's captain with all the people raising their glasses to him. This was a lovely gesture and when I made the decision to leave her, it made me feel guilty at letting her down but, nonetheless, I still think it was the right thing to do. I didn't feel in my mind and my heart that she was the right one for me. I think it was about 2004 when she died. At that time, I was still furious with her for killing Nicky, so I made her disappear. I turned her into a monkey as punishment for killing Nicky, and not giving much love to Anthony and Christopher. Maybe one day, if she wants to try again to be a good person, I will give her another chance and let her come back as a human again, but she has got a lot to do to impress me if she is worth another chance. I don't think I will be giving her one for a long time yet.

Minny Johnson was the REAL Queen of the Western World when she was alive. She was the one referred to in the kid's comic, *The Dandy*, as Minny the Minx. (Incidentally, *The Dandy* referred to me as 'Black Bob, the Dandy Wonder Dog.) There are many covert signs of Minny's dominance in western society. Such things as Mini cars, Miniskirts and Mini cabs, are all secret references to Minny Johnson. When President J.F. Kennedy was murdered, it was Lyndon Baines Johnson who became the next president. Many analysts into the death of JFK came to the conclusion that the best way to realise who really killed him is to look at who benefitted most from his death. I know that it is no coincidence that Lyndon Baines Johnson has the same surname as Minny. LBJ always was an allegorical figure for *her*. This is something that millions of Americans realised but because it was all secretive and couldn't be proven, no one had the guts to tell the truth.

Minny was the person who was really responsibly for the murder of JFK. *She* was the one who came to REAL power when JFK died. She became the REAL sexual and spiritual goddess of the Western World. She lived in a block of flats in Streatham, known as Sanders House. The many references to 'Golden Sands' in American culture are an indication the she was regarded as the Golden person, the number one, the REAL boss. What she wanted, she got. It was the leaders of the Soviet Union who accused the west of decadence and said that the leaders of the west were people who ate babies. The children in the west thought this was nonsense, but the adults knew it was the truth. The baby that Minny was eating was my dear son and the light of my life, Nicky. She and her followers were feeding sexually upon Nicky's spirit. They were the reason that Nicky was crying uncontrollably the night Jasmin 1 killed him. They were the ones who drove my stupid and weak wife to murder. Minny did what many gods are made to do and made a human sacrifice of her favourite child, her daughter, Iris. Minny was one of the most important influences in society who got me to kill Iris. When Minny died, I made her disappear. I turned her into an animal. An aardvark actually. That appealed to my sense of humour. The last thing she said was, and she said it to me, "You'll regret this." But I don't regret it and I don't think I ever will. She got the fitting punishment for her great sin of eating MY baby. I don't think the human race will ever hear from her again.

**Saturday 28th January 2017**. At the risk of repeating myself, I am now going to write about my attitude to homosexuality. Sodomy is a filthy and sordid act. It is highly offensive to the sensibilities of all decent people and we are fed up with having our faces rubbed into this filth by the media. It is not what a penis is for and it is not what an anus is for. It follows, therefore, that it is a perversion and shouldn't be allowed. Dolly was the leader. She was the one who, everybody accepted, had the power to seduce them, sexually and they all knew that, being what they are, there was nothing they could do about it.

It suited Dolly's fanciful notions to have sympathy for homosexuals and to take the attitude that they were people who should be allowed to pursue their filthy behaviour because they were adult people in a free society. But Dolly was not a good leader.

She was not a deep thinker and she lacked the awareness to realise that immorality was all part of Satan's plan to destroy humanity. People though, accepted that they must obey Dolly's will because she was the leader, even though it went against the better judgement of many of them. I say, consider this, what are homosexuals? They are not boys, for boys have yet to develop any sexuality, and they are not men, for men, by definition are people who are sexually attracted to women. This is a law of nature and only an idiot would disagree with it. I say again, they are not boys and they are not men, so what are they? I say the best word for them is 'queers'. Some of them say that it is the fault of me, God, for I made them what they are. I hear what these characters say and I concede they have a point but like some other things in life, people of good sense have found a purpose for them. Their purpose is to demonstrate to people what they should not be.

I have heard the thought that God is like a master potter, working at his wheel and that humans are like the works of pottery that he creates. Some of these pots are imperfect; either through defective clay, or imperfect workmanship. But even the wonky pots are still useable, usually, and there is a place for them. If, however, they want to live among us in society, they must accept responsibility for their own behaviour. Maybe they can't help being what they are but what they do about it is something they should learn to control. They should not practise offensive acts and if they do, I shall come down on them like a ton of bricks.

The institution of marriage is one which has served humanity well since the dawn of the human race on this planet.

It is a monogamous union of a man and a woman who love and care for each other. It cherishes the concept of sexual fidelity and is the highest form of relationship known to mankind. It is common to all societies in the world and is what has protected us since time immemorial and makes us better than animals. Its perversion to allow same sex marriage is another part of Satan's plan to destroy humanity by undermining the moral fabric of society. Dolly allowed it to happen because her ideas were not only fanciful and not only stupid, but WRONG. I want to see the laws allowing this wrong behaviour changed and things put right. I want this to happen in all societies where same sex marriages have been legitimised and I want it to happen soon. If the world does not do as I say, it will regret it. I repeat, I am the leader now and if you think about what I have been saying in my books, you will realise that you have no choice now but to accept my will.

I have two further thoughts to express. The first is about this word, 'homophobic'. I am not homophobic. A phobia is a fear of something. I am not afraid of homosexuals but those of them with any sense know damn well they should be afraid of me. When Dolly advocated the legitimising of homosexuality, people knew that I, God, considered it a sin and that I was against it. Many people must have thought that God was weak or ineffectual or unable to have His way. Now that MY will has triumphed over Dolly's, I am going to get my own way. It has taken a little time but events are now marching inexorably in my favour.

I am now going to write a bit about the spiteful nature of some women, especially sex goddesses. When women who are feted by society as sex symbols by such songs as *Living Doll* and *Hello Dolly,* this kind of adulation goes to their head and they think they can get away with anything. Especially women with strong willpower but of low moral fibre such as my mother, Dolly. I discovered the hard way the truth of that saying 'Hell hath no fury like a woman who's been scorned'. I rejected Dolly's sexual advances to me and her revenge on me for doing this was as follows: First she got her followers to drive me to homicide. I found this a horrible experience. It hurt my conscience and my opinion of myself. It went terribly against the grain with me but I had to accept that, if I was to prove I was a man, then this horrible job was one I had to do. Then she had me locked up in psychiatric hospitals for forty years. Most of this time in institutions of high security where I was treated like an animal. For almost all of this time I had horrible drugs injected into my backside against my will. This is one of the most heinous tortures known to mankind. The effects of these drugs are horrible in the extreme but these psychiatric bastards told me I needed them and that they were doing me good and that it was necessary to treat me this way, although they couldn't say why.

To add insult to injury, they labelled me with insulting and stigmatising epithets such as 'Mental Illness'. 'Paranoid Schizophrenia', 'Grandiose Delusions', 'Narcissism', and other horrible words too painful for me to remember.

I want it put on record that the only thing that was ever mentally ill about me was the fact that I refused to be a motherfucker.

To make matters worse, the horrible woman continued to pester me for sex, with her spirit, for a good ten years after she passed away. Not only that, but the spiteful woman even then continued to try and break up my relationship with the girl I love, my dear Lucy. I thank heaven that Lucy is strong enough and she cares enough for me to help me through it all. Lucy is also courageous enough to fight Dolly for me and, in the long run, she won, for it was only earlier this month that I finally managed to get rid of the evil pest who gave me birth and then tried to make me regret it ever since.

It is all over now. Dolly does not exist anymore and that is one of the greatest achievements of my life. I don't think I will be held in a mental hospital for much longer now. I have been off the drugs for over a month and I am rapidly recovering. My sex drive has returned and Lucy and I regularly make love with our minds and spirits. We 'dance' together in the sexual meaning of the word and climax together. I'm sure it won't be long now before we are together in body as well as in spirit and I'm now looking forward to a happy life with the most wonderful woman in the world.

I am now going to write some of my thoughts on psychiatry. A little while ago, my responsible clinician, Doctor Marionette Madre, wrote to us patients (or service users as they now like to call us) asking for our opinions as to what constitutes recovery from mental illness and how to tell those who are now mentally healthy. In truth, to decide who is now ready for society depends as much upon the nature of that society as it does upon the state of the patient. Society in the western world, for all my lifetime, has been one in which the identity of the REAL leader has been kept a secret. The REAL leadership of society is sexual and spiritual. The REAL leader is loved and revered as the living God. The leader's thoughts don't even have to be put into words to be known to their followers and obeyed. Their thoughts are transmitted telepathically and their power is absolute. In such a society, mental health is a question of knowing the identity of the leader and agreeing to keep it a secret. It is a matter of agreeing to follow the ways of the leader; their thoughts, attitudes and opinions, even though your own concepts may not be in agreement, you have to accept that you must swallow your pride and do as you are told, for your own sexual identity is consumed by that of the leader. You have to accept that they have seduced you sexually and there is now nothing you can do about it except to follow that person. That is what constitutes mental health in the kind of society that the west has been up until this month when I made Dolly disappear. In what I call a more natural society, the leader, the REAL God, has the courage, the honesty and the decency to let his people know who he (or she) is and to trust his people to protect him and both he and they live in happiness and security knowing who is really whom and who they are themselves. Not just mental, sexual and spiritual zombies who are not really themselves.

In this more natural society, mental health and mental illness are a question of sorting out the men from the boys. The responsible clinician has to know who has proven themselves and who hasn't yet. To do that they must be real adults themselves and that is where I can see problems arising. Over the forty plus years I have been in mental hospitals, I have been under no less that eighteen different psychiatrists. There was only one real man among them. All the others were immature, conceited, self-opinionated, egotistical idiots who had no idea of what real people are, had no understanding of life, nor of humanity, were not deep thinkers and had no knowledge of what is really important to people. They dispense drugs which have horrible effects on people without ever having taken them themselves, so they have no real knowledge of what they are really doing to people, nor how evil what they are doing really is.

The motto of the Royal College of Psychiatrists is, 'LET WISDOM PREVAIL'. This is a highly admirable sentiment but I must report that it is not lived up to by the practising practitioners of the profession. I have yet to meet a psychiatrist who I would consider to be a wise person. Most of them are mostly concerned with their cocktail parties, their own sex lives and their self-aggrandisement which they measure by what articles on their piffle they can get published in their professional journals.

I think their importance and influence in the British courts is wrongly placed. They are not the sort of people whose opinions I think deserve any credence at all. They are superficial and superfluous to society. They are parasites on the tax payer and a total waste of time and space.

This is what I think of psychiatrists. In short, the whole field of mental health is a mess because of the lack of courage, care and concern of the people whose job it is to sort things out. Many people who would, should and could be useful citizens are detained unnecessarily by people who do not really understand what is required of them and are not really up to the job of understanding human beings because they have never really lived themselves. As I say, the whole situation is a mess and I cannot see it improving in the foreseeable future. But enough of this rant of mine. Those who know what I have been through will know why I feel this way. I just hope they have what it takes to respect me for telling it like it is.

I am now going to write a few words on Islam. I don't know much about it but I do know that my spiritual identity is that of the Lord God himself. You know me as Allah. That is who I am. The big man himself. I have heard Muslims say Allah Akhba (God is great) and I want to thank you for having faith in my greatness. You who have read my words in this book will know that I truly am great. Your faith in me is not misplaced. I was born in England. That is where I came to life as a human being. But that does not mean that I am not Allah, the God of the Muslim people. I am the God of all people, all over the world. And my life is one of service to the human race. For the human race is MY creation. And I am here to protect and defend it. I have made Satan disappear. That is a measure of my greatness. He will never again trouble the human race. Some people call him 'The great Satan'. But I proved that he was not so great. Compared to me he was small.

I want to give you my opinion on the Prophet Muhammad and my reasons for this opinion. I believe he was not as strong as he should have been and he did not know the will of Allah as well as he should have done if he was to claim to be the messenger of Allah. I will now tell you why I say these things, so men of reason can judge for themselves what the truth is and make up their own minds what to believe. He allowed himself to be seduced, sexually, by women he was not married to. That is why I call him weak. He ended up with four wives, which is not the will of Allah. It is the will of Allah that men and women should follow the ideals of monogamy and fidelity. For a man and woman who follow these ideals and really love each other are enjoying the highest spiritual form of relationship known to mankind. That is what I, Allah, want for all my people. That is my will and I want it known to everybody. I am now here in person to tell you my will, so that nobody has to rely upon the opinion of imperfect messengers in future.

To conclude this chapter, I am going to write about my future; what I hope for and expect. I have said before that I think I have at least another thirty years of life left in me, for although I am seventy-three years old at the moment, I am made of extremely good stuff and I fully expect to prove myself right. I am hoping for and I feel sure I will have an extremely happy marriage to my dear Lucy, the woman I love, and my soulmate. I intend to have and enjoy a happy retirement and I am still hoping for some success as a songwriter and possibly also an inventor, if my idea for a Thermal Electricity Generator works. I still intend to pursue my claim for justice for myself. I have said before and I will say again that I want four things: FREEDOM, APOLOGY, EXONERATION AND COMPENSATION. I will not elaborate again on these things. I have done so already many times in my writings. What I am asking for is not just a modest claim, it is trivial compared to my worth to the community, which people who have read my books will know and understand. I am not anticipating much resistance to my claims. When I get my compensation money I will be able to live myself and also my dear wife, Lucy, in the style to which we aspire. We are not greedy people, nor are we snobs, but we are people of good taste and who want and feel we deserve some of the good things in life. I don't think that we will have to strive too hard in future to get the things we want. I am sure that we will both live with the love, goodwill and respect of our fellow citizens, for they are good people and I know they will prove to us that they are worthy of all the things we have done for them.

That's all I have to say for now. It brings the reader up to date with my story, and it may be some time from now before I do more writing. Thank you for reading my books. I hope you found them interesting and enlightening and I hope that they will have helped you in your life. Live a good life and go with my blessing.

Robert Brooks Strong.

CPSIA information can be obtained
at www.ICGtesting.com
Printed in the USA
BVHW030941030719
552580BV00011B/848/P